DOING THE TWIST

to

AMAZING GRACE

Alice Ogden Bellis

DOING THE TWIST
to
AMAZING GRACE

THE PILGRIM PRESS
CLEVELAND, OHIO

The Pilgrim Press, Cleveland, Ohio 44115
© 1998 by Alice Ogden Bellis

Biblical quotations are from the New Revised Standard Version of
the Bible, © 1989 by the Division of Christian Education of the
National Council of the Churches of Christ in the U.S.A., and are
used by permission.

Printed in the United States of America on acid-free paper

03   02   01   00   99   98   5   4   3   2   1

Library of Congress Cataloging-in-Publication Data

Bellis, Alice Ogden, 1950–
    Doing the twist to amazing grace / Alice Ogden Bellis.
        p.   cm.
    Includes bibliographical references.
    ISBN 0-8298-1273-3 (paper : alk. paper)
    1. Theology, Doctrinal—Popular works.   2. Presbyterian
Church (U.S.A.)—Doctrines.   I. Title.
BT77.B415   1998
234—dc21   98-36256
                                                                 CIP

For

MARGARET

and

ELIZABETH

· Contents ·

· *Acknowledgments* ·

*T*his book might never have been published if not for the encouragement and assistance of David Bittinger, who read an early version of the manuscript, advised me on matters of writing style, and offered suggestions about what to keep and what to cut. His enthusiasm for the project helped me believe in it and persist in completing it.

An equally important partner in this project has been my husband, Douglass Bellis, who has read this manuscript at least twice and has also given me important suggestions as to both style and substance.

I also thank my colleague Michael Willett Newheart, associate professor of New Testament at Howard Divinity School, whose advice on matters of New Testament scholarship that are touched on in this book allayed my fears about venturing into waters outside my area of academic expertise.

Special thanks go to Howard University School of Divinity, which allowed me a sabbatical leave to complete this and other projects. To all those teachers, students, family, and friends, both within and outside the institutional church, who have helped me sort through the religious questions addressed in this book, I express my sincere appreciation.

I express appreciation also to the many people whom I have never met in person but whose books and articles I have read over a lifetime, who have in ways both subtle and profound shaped the convictions expressed in this book. I cannot possibly acknowledge them all, nor even list all of them in the additional resources provided at the end of each chapter.

I have avoided the use of any textual notes, trying to keep the text unencumbered so as not to distract general readers with scholarly paraphernalia. Some books listed at the end of each chapter were ones I found after I had completed the text and included because they seemed to be helpful resources. However, in one case I am especially indebted to an author for an idea that I used. Bruce Chilton's *Bible Review* article listed at the end of chapter 3 shaped my thinking on Holy Communion.

· *Introduction* ·

A FULLY EXAMINED FAITH

I grew up in the Bible Belt. My life was centered in two institutions, the church and the public school system. Fairly early in life, these two centers of my life began to fight with each other. The fight was not out in the open; the battles were fought within my own psyche. It was not that my teachers opposed the church; to the contrary, they were churchgoing people just like my family. Yet the value of reason that I learned in school and that was reinforced by my parents, who encouraged me to do well in school, was subtly but powerfully in conflict with the sort of theology that I learned at church.

Some of my friends who experienced this same conflict have long since ceased to be involved in any church. They resolved the conflict in favor of reason. I could not leave behind either of the two institutions that shaped my innermost being. Nor could I live my life as a spiritual schizophrenic. I had to find a way to reconcile the truths of both church and academia.

When I went to college, planning to major in English literature and to get a teaching certificate so that I could teach high school English, I was following in the footsteps of my favorite high school teacher, who had a tremendous impact on me. However, when I arrived at college and signed up to take an introduction to Old Testament course in my first semester, my plans were poised to be altered dramatically. For the first time in my life, my religious questions were taken seriously. I received tools with which I could begin to address the inner conflicts that tormented me. Ultimately, I switched to a religion major without any idea of where it might lead. I felt that college was the place to become educated. Careers were of secondary concern at that point.

In my senior year in college, my vocational plans emerged. Although I had never met a woman minister in my life and was only vaguely aware that the Presbyterian church ordained women, it became quite clear to me that some form of ministry was my "call." As a child I had wanted to marry a minister like my Uncle John, a Presbyterian minister whom I admired greatly. As I grew older I put away this childish notion. It was only in my last year of college that the childhood fantasy reemerged, but I realized that I was not supposed to marry a minister; I was supposed to become one myself.

In divinity school I continued my search to sort out my religious questions. Even by the end of divinity school, I was not fully satisfied, and so I went to graduate school to get a

Ph.D. in Semitic languages, with a major in Hebrew. During these years of intense study of biblical texts and Semitic languages related to Hebrew, the most serious of my questions were answered. After I completed the course work, I began work as an associate minister at a suburban Presbyterian church, where I experienced, from the other side, some of the same types of theology that I had learned as a child.

When the invitation came to teach at the same seminary I had attended, I was delighted. I had loved teaching adults in the church context, but much of my time was necessarily devoted to other tasks. Now I could do full-time what I loved best, teaching and writing. The two institutions that had been the focus of my youth are now equally a part of my life, but this time there is no conflict. Reason and religion join hand in hand.

Yet, having finally found peace, I cannot rest. I know that the struggles that I have experienced are not mine alone. Although none of our life stories is identical, some of what I have experienced is shared by others. My commitment to the church, in the broadest sense of the term, and to others who are seeking the light of religious truth has inspired me to share my story and some of the convictions that I have gained as I have sought to make sense out of the various legacies bequeathed to me.

· One ·

DOING THE TWIST TO AMAZING GRACE

*I*n the seventh grade I made a difficult choice between continuing ballet classes and taking ballroom dance. All my friends, it seemed, were signing up for ballroom, and I did not want to be left out. In many ways I ended up regretting dropping ballet, because the ballroom class was boring. We learned the fox-trot and bossa nova and cha-cha, dances I have never done since. We also learned the jitterbug, which was the reigning style at the time in my part of the South, but it is such a simple dance that it could be learned in a few minutes.

The most memorable part of the class was learning that year's dance, the twist. I can vividly remember dancing to Chubby Checker and finding the new style refreshing and fun. I still like the twist and do it regularly in aerobics classes that I teach. It's great for the waistline!

Of course, I have never done the twist to the hymn "Amazing Grace" and cannot imagine trying to combine these two very different moods. "Amazing Grace" has been one of my favorite hymns ever since my last year in college, when Judy Collins popularized it. My husband (then just a friend) and I used to sing it together, accompanied by my guitar and his dulcimer. It is one of the few hymns of which I know all the verses by heart.

The hymn articulates a very basic theology—that it is God's grace that sets us free, changes our blindness to sight, and finds us in our lostness. Though I am a child of the church, I identify very much with this theology. God found me in my lostness, opened my eyes, set me free. I was lost in confusion, unable to make sense out of the theology that permeated my culture. God took pity on me and helped me find the answers that I craved. Only God's grace could work such miracles.

Unfortunately, this simple theology tempts us to tamper with it, to tangle it, to twist it. We do not like to admit that we need God. We do not like to acknowledge that without God's help we are helpless. We want control over our spiritual lives.

We are ably assisted in our maneuverings by a power that we sometimes call the devil or Satan. I do not believe in the literal reality of a man in a red suit with horns and a pitchfork, but I do believe that this poetic imagery of the devil expresses a profound truth that an evil power is at work in the world. Sometimes this power almost seems to have a personality, something real and concrete in its evil presence and its potency.

The kind of liberal Christianity that is prevalent in many mainline denominations prefers to ignore this underside of reality, finding it more pleasant to rhapsodize about God's love. God's love is, of course, the ultimate reality, but it is fully grasped only when we appreciate how that divine love is engaged in a battle with the forces of evil. Perhaps that is why those who have suffered most are sometimes most acutely aware of the love of God.

The devil—or the reality that the term "devil" represents—loves nothing better than to twist God's truth into a parody of itself. The parody still looks something like the real thing—just as we can still recognize ourselves in the strange reflections we see in wavy mirrors at beach pavilions—but the essence has been perverted. We can see the way this works if we reflect on Judeo-Christian history.

God called the Hebrews out of Egyptian bondage to be a special people. God called them into a new social order in which the needs of all, including the orphans, widows, and sojourners, would be considered. It did not take long, however, before God had to send prophets and teachers to call the people back to the vision.

Amos and Micah reminded the people that God was concerned about what we today call social justice. Isaiah and Jeremiah called the people to trust in God, not in politics. They were not arguing, as some do today, that religion and politics don't mix; they were against what we call realpolitik. In addition, Jeremiah lambasted the people for their shallow theology and their idolatrous attitudes toward the Jerusalem Temple that they believed God would preserve regardless of their behavior. It was too late, however, for disaster to be averted. God allowed the Babylonians to destroy the Temple and capital city and to exile the elite citizens to faraway Babylon.

After the Exile, when the Jews expelled foreign women and built spiritual walls around themselves to preserve their identity, the author of the book of Ruth subtly undercut the Jerusalem establishment's bias against foreign women. The author of the book of Esther criticized those who believed that the Jews in the Diaspora were of less value than those at home. The book of Jonah reminds us that God loves everyone, even our worst enemies. In a similar way Jesus criticized the Jerusalem establishment of his day for its shallow, conventional theology and its immoral behavior. He focused instead on God's love for everyone, including the people considered outcasts in his community.

God sent Martin Luther and John Calvin and many other reformers to bring people back to the basic truth that God's amazing grace is the only way to salvation, to health and wholeness. In our own century God sent Martin Luther King Jr. to convict us of our national sin of racism and to bring us back to the truth that we are all equally God's children.

Sadly, we are slow learners. We would rather try to buy our salvation, clutch at superficial differences to support obscure hatreds, and live lives marked by vacuity and boredom relieved only by the shallow excitement of televised violence. The devil is a clever fellow who loves nothing better than doing the twist to God's amazing grace.

The Reformed tradition of Protestantism understands itself to be always in need of further reformation. Certainly, the churches are now in need of God's reforming spirit. The Spirit is clearly blowing. Whether the result will be the renewal or the extinction of some denominations is hard to say. Churches not open to being reformed will surely wither, and God will plant new shoots in more fertile ground. Whatever happens, I revel in God's amazing grace, a power capable of redeeming even the most lost and myopic humans, the most lost and shortsighted institutions.

JOHN 3:16

On a tree-lined street in a medium-sized town in the Piedmont section of North Carolina, a quiet city block is occupied by an elegant neocolonial ecclesiastical structure of the type that was popular in the 1950s among affluent Presbyterians. In this complex many years ago, I happily walked down a polished linoleum corridor leading to a classroom every Sunday morning at ten o'clock. I wore a pretty dress made by my mother and shiny patent leather shoes with little white socks. I carried a small purse in which I had carefully placed a dime, the tithe of my weekly allowance that would be collected during the class.

On one of the bulletin boards was an attendance poster provided by the denomination, where weekly attendance and absence were carefully noted. On another board was a second poster, this one handmade, on which the names of the members of the church school class filled the left side of the poster and biblical passages to be memorized were inscribed across the top. As these passages were successfully recited, a star or a check mark was placed in the appropriate box. Many checks and stars could be seen beside my name.

The teachers were mostly women, but one man, a tall, gaunt World War II concentration camp survivor, was a cheerful presence in the classroom. The ministers, rarely seen in the children's classrooms, were older men, but a vivacious young woman was the director of Christian education.

On a corridor parallel to the one on which the elementary schoolchildren's classrooms were housed, the younger children went to their nursery and preschool rooms. So well stocked with toys was the preschool room that older children often begged to be allowed to help with the younger children in order to avoid church attendance and, equally important, to play with the toys they supposedly had outgrown. Especially memorable was the collection of wooden blocks out of which cities and even empires could be constructed by aspiring young builders and architects.

The sanctuary of the church had deep red carpeting, white walls, and pews and pulpit furniture that combined dark varnished wood and white painted wood. There were no stained glass windows, but the dark wood and brass candlesticks added warmth to the room. A pipe organ and a harpsichord were played by the organist-choirmaster, an accomplished musician. (To this day he continues to provide musical direction to the church.) He led the many choirs— the adult choir with paid soloists, the junior and carol choirs composed of upper and lower elementary schoolchildren, and the handbell choir in which older children played. On special occasions guest musicians would come—trumpeters, kettledrummers, harpists, and cellists.

The chapel had beautiful blue carpeting and was similar to the large sanctuary except on a much smaller scale. Here the early worship services before church school were held, and here the communicants' class met each week to receive instruction from the minister before formally joining the church.

The church was also equipped with an institutional kitchen, from which large dinners were served. On Wednesday nights during the school year, families came to a potluck supper at which the children enjoyed filling their plates many times over. Concoctions oozing with sour cream, hamburger, and noodles were followed by delectable desserts.

As children grew into teenagers, they were invited to come back to church on Sunday evenings for youth meetings that were also somewhat social in nature. Occasional retreats to a lake cottage or the beach would include opportunities for recreation and minimal study.

I sang in the choir, played handbells, and participated in Christmas pageants, Easter sunrise services, youth retreats, and all the rest. My parents were and still are pillars of the church.

It is strange, the things we remember from childhood. I remember little about the communicants' class except that it met one afternoon after school each week for a series of weeks and that I surreptitiously ate Baby Ruth candy bars during the class in the lovely chapel.

I also recall taking my first communion at the end of the course on a Maundy Thursday evening (the Thursday night before Easter, on which Jesus celebrated the Last Supper with his disciples). It was not until years later that I learned that Maundy Thursday received its name from the Latin for *mandate,* because Jesus gave his disciples a new commandment, to love one another, on this night.

For this communion I was all dressed up, as was the custom for the girls, in a white dress. After waiting so long for this event, I was somewhat disappointed that a mystical experience did not accompany the sacrament. I thought there would at least be more to it than what happened at that particular worship service. Perhaps if I had listened more closely during the classes, I would have been better prepared!

I remember people, places, and events, but only one biblical interpretation from those early days of church life has remained with me. I do not even remember which pastor or teacher(s) first introduced this tight knot of theological threads to me. Nevertheless, this knot became bound up with the fabric of my life and took years for me to untie.

The biblical text was the famous John 3:16, "For God so loved the world that he gave his only Son, so that everyone who believes in him may not perish but may have eternal life." That's the New Revised Standard Version. What I heard as a child was surely the Revised Standard Version, since that was the Bible that white Protestants favored in the 1950s, when I was growing up.

The meaning of this passage was conveyed to me subtly but powerfully: Jesus is God and if you accept this equation, then God gives you your ticket to heaven. Was that really what was taught or merely what I understood? My subsequent experience has led me to believe that I correctly understood what was being taught and properly doubted that such tickets were readily issued.

It took me many years of college and seminary religion courses to understand that what I was taught as a child was not John 3:16 pure and simple, but a badly mangled version of it. However, I learned when I later served as a minister that what I had been taught, as twisted as I now believe it to be, is a common understanding of the passage, at least among a significant segment of Protestant Americans.

This common misreading identifies faith (believing in Jesus) with credulity, that is, unquestioning acceptance of a doctrine. According to this interpretation, faith is believing what is otherwise un-believable. This approach to faith expects believers to accept a doctrine about which they understand nothing or almost nothing. This "faith" affirms something that under other cir-cumstances would seem absurd.

Questions are discouraged by those who define faith this way. Often such people reverently intone the words "It's a mystery," as if that settled the matter. In fact, in New Testa-ment Greek, the word *mysterion* means something wonder-ful that God has *revealed.* This biblical definition is precisely the opposite of the popularly accepted one. How the devil loves to twist the truth.

An Episcopal church in the Chicago area responded to this pervasive error with a poster on which a traditional pic-ture of a crucified Christ appeared. The caption beneath the picture read, "Jesus died to take away our sins, not our minds."

It is certainly true that we humans cannot know every-thing we would like to know about God and God's ways. But God has revealed much about the divine reality to humans who have eyes to see, ears to hear, and a mind to learn. I have experienced God at work in my life and in the lives of oth-ers. Thus I put my faith—that is, my trust—in the God whom I have seen and heard and experienced, if only dimly.

Although I have come to know and love God in part be-cause of the way God's truth and wisdom are revealed in the Bible, I do not *equate* God's Word with the Bible. Although

I don't believe in inerrancy, the belief that the Scriptures contain no errors (see the section "The Trouble with Translations" in chapter 3), I do hear God's Word as I study and reflect on the stories and teaching in the Bible.

This knowledge does not resemble scientific knowledge that makes various technologies possible, important as these are in the modern world. Religious knowledge is closer to the kind of knowledge we gain when we read T. S. Eliot's *The Wasteland* or the kind of inspiration we feel when we hear a Bach concerto or view the ballet *Swan Lake.* Experiences such as these shape us in ways that are not reducible to numbers and facts. Of course, the greatest scientists have always understood that there is far more to science than equations. Albert Einstein's reverence for the deity responsible for the universe is evidence of the way all dimensions of life point us to the reality of God.

So, the first of the threads twisted together in the knotty interpretation of John 3:16 that I learned is the faulty identification of faith with credulity. The second thread is the simplistic identification of Jesus, God's child, with God the Father or, as we might less anthropomorphically call the first person of the Trinity, the Creator.

The doctrine of the Trinity is very difficult for contemporary Westerners to grasp, in part because it is based on classical Greek modes of thought to which we are not accustomed, and in part because one of the Latin words into which the original Greek was translated has entered English in a translation that obscures the original intention.

The doctrine of the Trinity was a postbiblical attempt to describe the simultaneous truth of two seemingly contradictory realities: that God is one and that God manifests the divine nature in a multiplicity of ways. The Greek word used to express God's many aspects or guises was *prosopon,* literally "face." Of course, God does not really have three faces, or any faces, for that matter. God has no physical face(s) at all, because God is spirit. However, God does manifest the divine presence in many ways or, to use a metaphor, in many faces. In modern English we might say that God wears many hats.

In Latin the word used to translate *prosopon* was *persona.* Roman actors would don various masks or *personae* to represent different characters they were playing in a drama. Indeed, some plays are still put on today with only one actor, who keeps running behind a prop to put on a different hat or other identifying piece of clothing for each character represented.

Unfortunately, when *persona* was translated into English, the word chosen as its equivalent was the similar-sounding but different-meaning "person." The English phrase "God in three persons" suggests that God consists of three separate personalities, each of equal weight, power, and authority. Some eighteenth- and nineteenth-century American theologians spoke of the Trinity as if it were composed of three separate gods who carried on conversations with and had an emotional relationship to one another. Such views lost God's oneness in the attempt to describe God's "plurality."

The Christians who ultimately were called Unitarians reacted negatively to this kind of theology, and a religious movement was born. Because of the modern Christian tendency toward what amounts to tritheism, or the worship of three gods (Father, Son, and Holy Ghost), I am sometimes more comfortable in Unitarian settings than in trinitarian ones. In trinitarian circles I often sound Unitarian, because I feel the need to hold up the truth of God's unity, but in Unitarian circles I usually sound trinitarian, because I also believe in the special nature of God's manifestation in Jesus.

Christians often think that Unitarians are not Christian, and certainly many Unitarians do not identify themselves as such. There is nothing in Unitarianism, however, that is antithetical to Christian faith. Unitarianism is the direct descendant of New England Puritanism, which thought that creeds were dangerous. To this day the Unitarians do not have a creed, though some of their denominational statements come close. A person can be a trinitarian theologically and belong to a Unitarian church. Those with affinities for Judaism and Buddhism can also join a Unitarian church. All that one must agree to do in order to join a Unitarian church is to seek religious truth.

In any case, the doctrine of the Trinity is not biblical. It is postbiblical, composed by men trying to make sense of their religious experiences. The popular American understanding of the Trinity is a gross distortion of the original doctrine. This distortion is read back into John 3:16 as if it *were* John 3:16. This twisted interpretation then becomes a substitute for what the author was saying in John 3:16.

The original formulators of the Trinity were correct to try to find a way to hold together God's unity and diversity. The history of this doctrine, however, is ample evidence of how much the devil loves to do the twist to God's amazing grace. God is one, but we experience God in many ways. One of the most important ways Christians have experienced God's powerful presence is in the biblical stories of the life of Jesus of Nazareth.

God was surely at work in Jesus in a wonderfully unique way. Jesus extended God's love to those who were considered religiously unacceptable. He challenged the conventional religiosity of his day, parodied the religious elite in parables such as that of the good Samaritan, and taught that the first shall be last and the last first. He taught the possibility of having a personal relationship with God and the inadequacy of merely following the rules.

We can use many poetic expressions to give utterance to the sublime truth of Jesus' life: Immanuel, which means in Hebrew "God with us"; Son or Child of God, which means having the characteristics of God; Messiah, which means "the anointed one" in Hebrew; and Christ, which is the Greek for Messiah. These are all true expressions, but none allows us to go the additional step of calling Jesus God. Jesus always pointed *beyond* himself to God.

The second person of the Trinity, God's Word or Logos (in Greek literally "word," but also meaning reason and rationality and, in the New Testament context, divine reason), was made flesh in Jesus. This expression is also poetry, but it attempts to express the reality that the disciples experienced when they were with Jesus, feeling they were in the presence of God, especially God's reason or wisdom.

Jesus felt at times very close to God, but he never made the mistake of equating himself with the Creator. Neither did the biblical authors. John could speak of the Word of God being God and of the Word of God becoming flesh in Jesus (John 1:1, 14), coming perhaps as close as any biblical words do to equating God with Jesus, but they do not make this equation.

It is not enough for the devil to persuade us to make the false identifications of faith with credulity and of Jesus with the Creator. The third thread woven in the popular misinterpretation of John 3:16 is the one that ties the knot tightly. The third thread is dependent on the first two. Once faith has been replaced with credulity and Jesus oversimplistically identified with the Creator, then it is a fairly simple matter to define salvation as the result of "faith" (really credulity) in "God" (really Jesus' divinity). After all, wasn't that what the Protestant Reformation was all about: justification (salvation) by faith?

At the time of the Reformation, the Roman Catholics emphasized the importance of doing good works for salvation. Martin Luther was profoundly disturbed by the gnawing sense that he could never do enough good deeds to earn his way into heaven. Finally, after much Bible study, prayer, and reflection, he came to the conviction that we could be saved not by good works but only by faith in the biblical sense, that is, by a relationship of trust with God. The truth of his personal breakthrough was the catalyst that began the Reformation. There was, of course, much more to Luther's theology, but his concept of salvation through faith is what is essential for this discussion.

The problem is that faith in God as understood by Luther is a far cry from the superficial credulity and polytheistic Christology of modern popular Christianity. The Reformation conviction was that a deep and abiding trust in the one God is the only thing in the world that can make life whole, which is what salvation does. The Greek word *so-terion,* "salvation," literally means "health and wholeness."

A deep sense of trust in God is life-transforming. A shallow belief in what seems utterly absurd is worse than useless. It is superstition, the devil's tool. Real faith does not come easily. It is not something we can will into existence. I can decide to believe in the theory of relativity, even if I do not have the faintest notion of what it means. However, such "faith" does not affect me in any significant way. For all practical purposes, I might as well reject relativity. Although I can decide to accept relativity, I cannot will to understand it any more than I can will to trust in God.

Real faith involves the conviction that God is real and that God loves us in spite of our weakness and stupidity and folly. When we are at our most honest, most of us do not feel worthy. We cannot change that sense of unworthiness. Only God can break through and give us the sense of self-worth for which we yearn. Nurturing environments can help and God works through human beings, but humans can never engineer an environment that will guarantee the self-critical self-esteem that is basic to happiness.

There are perhaps ways we can open ourselves to God's amazing grace, but only God can shower that life-transforming "substance" on us, give us trust, and make us whole and happy. That is why the biblical authors emphasized that faith is a free gift. We cannot and need not try to earn it, buy it, or make it happen.

Salvation is not, as the cynical old saw goes, "pie in the sky by and by." It includes a sense of well-being in the present, whatever our temporal circumstances may be. Circumstances may test our trust of God, may make us question God's justice and/or mercy, and may surely make life trying. But trust in God is stronger than the chains of prison, more powerful than the bonds of slavery, and mightier than the whip, the sword, or the lion. Riches, comfort, power, even safety are not the final goals of life, so the lack of them, though not desirable, is not the worst possible fate. The lack of a relationship with God is the worst possible fate, even if one has riches, power, comfort, and safety.

The experiences of many African Americans testify to this. What people has suffered more yet produced such exemplars of faith as Martin Luther King Jr. and countless others well known and obscure? As a result of both their experience of slavery and their introduction to the Bible, African Americans came to identify with the Hebrew people whom God liberated from Egyptian bondage. They found hope in a God who returned God's people from Babylonian exile. They could identify with a suffering Jesus and celebrate his resurrection.

It is ironic that sometimes those who have suffered most trust in God the most strongly. Their lack of money, power, prestige, security, and comfort may push them to find their security in God. There is no guarantee of this, but it can and does happen. The trust in God that such people develop then helps them endure the hardships of life. It teaches them that they are human beings created in God's image, even if other humans will not acknowledge this. Credulity can never provide a shield against the blows that life sometimes sends our way. Trust in God can.

It is also true that people who have everything the world can offer sometimes realize how empty it is without a relationship with God. Such people sometimes experience dramatic conversions accompanied by a new direction in life. Just as poverty does not guarantee a relationship with God, neither does wealth. Frequently wealth is a stumbling block. That is why Jesus said that it is harder for a rich person to enter the dominion of heaven than for a camel to go through the eye of a needle (Matt. 19:24; Mark 10:25), though he added that with God all things are possible (Matt. 19:26; Mark 10:27). Thus, neither poverty nor wealth is a requirement for or a guarantor of a relationship with God. God reaches out to people in all circumstances of life.

ATONEMENT

About three miles outside the beltway that circles Washington, D.C., on a major commuter route sits a salmon-colored brick church complex designed in a style typical of the 1960s. Like the older, more stately building in which I went to church as a child, though not so large or elegant, this building includes a sanctuary, fellowship hall, kitchen, and educational wing.

The sanctuary is the most recent and most attractive part of the building. Large, clear windows illumine the room brightly. The unstained oak pews, pulpit furniture, neo-Gothic arches, and teal green carpeting also contribute to the sense of lightness. A stained glass window of the tree of life is the focal point. Fixtures include a computerized electronic organ and a grand piano. Families gather on Sunday mornings for church school and church, choirs rehearse and teenagers gather at various times during the week, and social events occur sporadically. In addition, the building is used extensively throughout the week for church meetings and meetings of many outside groups, such as Alcoholics Anonymous.

On one Good Friday evening I rushed into the church to take my place in the worship service. It was a rainy night, and the church was unusually somber, the cross draped with black fabric. Scriptures were read, prayers prayed, and hymns such as "Sacred Head Now Wounded" sung mournfully. After the service, the worshipers left silently without greeting the ministers or one another as they normally would do on a Sunday morning.

I experienced a number of these so-called Good Friday services. Being one of the ministers, I could not just stay home; I was a participant. But I dreaded these funereal events. I had grown accustomed to Maundy Thursday services that commemorate Jesus' Last Supper, which, though somber, were a little more upbeat. Good Friday seemed to me excruciatingly morbid. The tone of such services reminded me of the rubbernecking that accompanies any major accident on the highway. There is something unwholesome about the way popular Christianity focuses on Jesus' death.

If I had difficulty swallowing the twisted version of John 3:16 that was and is current among many churchgoers, I had even greater problems accepting theories of atonement (how we are saved). The standard theories all focus on Jesus' death. These theories of atonement are biblically based and include sacrifice, ransom, and redemption, all from the Hebrew Scriptures (Old Testament). Drawing from various motifs in the Hebrew Bible, the New Testament authors sought ways of making sense of Jesus' death.

Since sacrifices in the Temple were such an important part of Hebrew worship, it was logical to think of Jesus' death as the supreme sacrifice. He was called the Lamb of God because, like the sacrifice of lambs at Passover to ward off the angel of death, Jesus' death was understood to ward off spiritual death.

In the same way that a person sold into slavery could be ransomed by a relative who paid a big enough price, it also made sense to equate the large price Jesus paid when he gave up his life with a ransom paid to buy sinners back from the power of sin. The term "redemption" originally was similar to "ransom." The redeemer was the next of kin who had the obligation to redeem the land of a relative that had been sold to pay off debts. The redeemer also was expected to redeem the life of a relative who had been sold into slavery. So Jesus could easily be understood as the redeemer who had redeemed his spiritual brothers and sisters from bondage to sin and death.

Understood poetically, these images of sacrifice, ransom, and redemption are quite beautiful. Understood literally, beyond the realm of poetry, we have to ask how Jesus' death helps the problem of sinful humanity.

Perhaps before trying to make sense of atonement, we should think about the human condition. Most people would probably agree that humans have many problems. We are greedy, jealous, contentious, and selfish (to name just a few of our shortcomings). Most of us experience life as less than we imagine it should be.

At times we glimpse the way things are supposed to be when humans are loving and caring, as, for example, when a sudden, intense snowstorm brings out the best in everyone. Much of the time, though, humans are cruelly and coarsely competitive. Most of us would agree that this is not the way life ought to be. We also know that even when we try to do unto others as we would have them do unto us, we often fail. In short, we need help.

Christians believe that Jesus somehow provides a solution to this problem. The usual understandings short-circuit Jesus' life and teaching, focusing instead on his divine nature and his death. Because Jesus is seen as a divine being who willingly gave up his life, this sacrifice is somehow supposed to solve humanity's sin problem.

But what does Jesus' death change? The causality of this supposition is as shaky as it is fervent. Even if one accepts the equation of Jesus with God, how does God's sacrifice solve humanity's problem? Neither God's benevolence nor human "faith" seems an adequate solution. There must be something more. Of course, there is: the life that Jesus led, the very life that led to his death at human hands, a life that triumphed over death and so undermines death's dominion over us, as well as the tyranny of society that can choke our lives, literally or figuratively.

Perhaps popular inherited theology bypasses Jesus' life and teaching because that life and teaching might require or inspire us to change the way we live and the way we think. It is more comforting to think that Jesus died for our sins and paid our ransom in full, and that all we have to do is believe that he was God to make the magic work.

In reality it is clear from the biblical record that Jesus came to challenge the comfortable and to comfort the oppressed. The theologically comfortable in his day were not so different from the theologically comfortable today. In Jesus' day religious security for some came, in part, from following a prescribed set of laws. The gift of the law, which Jews were supposed to follow *in response* to God's grace, apparently became for some a means to attain righteousness. Similarly, today religious security for some Christians comes from paying lip service to certain doctrines, often in rituals on Sunday. In neither case are those who are members of the religious establishment required to examine themselves. It is often more important to espouse the right theology, give money to the church, teach church school, and serve on committees, or maybe to help in soup kitchens and do good works for an alien poor.

Jesus came to teach us that real security, real wholeness, real salvation come not from merely doing what conventional religiosity seems to require (in his day, meticulously following the rules; in our day, belonging to the right church and believing and doing the things that the church encourages us to do). In fact, salvation comes from something much more important but also much more elusive.

Both the Hebrew Bible and the New Testament make clear that what gives life meaning is, first of all, trusting in God's love for us. (Contrary to popular opinion, the Hebrew Bible is not primarily a book of law to be contrasted with a grace-filled New Testament.) The self-esteem that comes from the trust in God that is taught in both testaments enables us to meet the indignities that the world heaps on us without losing our self-respect. It also enables us in some cases to change for the better those who would oppress us.

When we refuse to accept their contempt for us and at the same time refuse to return their contempt, then they may stop for a moment and take notice. In this way we may be part of God's activity in the world. The self-esteem that comes from trust in God also enables us to address our own failures and begin to correct them.

God is constantly bringing the high and mighty down and raising up the dregs of society. God is in the business of doing justice and dispensing mercy. God is spreading truth and love in a world in which these commodities are scarce. Trusting in God's love for us frees us from running after salvation in all the wrong places and allows us to become part of what God is doing in the world.

Most people seek meaning in life through money. We think that if we have enough money, people will respect us and then we can respect ourselves. Money is not evil, but money cannot buy us happiness. A famous proverb reads as follows:

> *Happy are those who find wisdom,*
> *   and those who get understanding,*
> *for her income is better than silver,*
> *   and her revenue better than gold. (Prov. 3:13–14)*

A few verses later we read these lines:

> *Her [wisdom's] ways are ways of pleasantness,*
> *   and all her paths are peace.*
> *She is a tree of life to those who lay hold of her;*
> *   those who hold her fast are called happy. (vv. 17–18)*

Of course, biblical wisdom is not mere intellectual knowledge; it is reverence for and trust in God.

In a similar vein Jesus said, "Strive first for the kingdom of God and his righteousness, and all these things will be given to you as well" (Matt. 6:33). Most of us reverse the priorities. We seek "all these things" first, and with whatever time and energy is left over, we seek the "kingdom." Then we wonder why life seems so hollow.

The only real power is God's, and the hollowly religious of our time are as loath to admit this as were the hollowly religious of Jesus' time. The only way to be part of something really enduring is to be part of God's action. And the only way to be part of God's action is to put that reality in front of everything else.

In one very real sense Jesus did not say anything fundamental that had not already been said before in the Hebrew Scriptures. When asked what was the greatest law, he quoted the Shema (pronounced she-MAH) from Deuteronomy: "Hear O Israel: The Lord is our God, the Lord alone. You shall love the Lord your God with all your heart, and with all your soul, and with all your might" (6:4–5). The name Shema comes from the first word of this passage in Hebrew, "Hear." The second law Jesus gave was similar and is from the book of Leviticus: "You shall love your neighbor as yourself" (19:18b).

Yet in every age people turn away from the simple truth and construct complex systems of theology and law to protect themselves from it. Jesus saw through this flight of distraction in his age, and we must see through it in ours. The particulars are different, but the principle is the same. The search for simplicity in religion is one element of reform throughout history. We will return to the place of law in religion later.

Jesus was full of God's Spirit. He saw the shallowness of his day and challenged it, just as the prophets had done before him. He spent his time with the outcasts of his day—the tax collectors, the "bad" women, the Samaritans. He found them much better company than the respectable people. If Jesus were among us today, would he spend time in our churches, or would he be found among the prostitutes, the gay community, the homeless, and the drug addicts? Some of these groups have serious problems, but they are not hypocrites.

What are the implications of Jesus' spending time with such people? Jesus' convictions about God's love for people regardless of their fitness according to traditional formulas brought him into serious conflict with both the religious authorities and the Roman political authorities. Ultimately Jesus' convictions led to his death. He probably would not have died if he had minded his own business and not meddled with conventional wisdom. He was playing with fire and got burned; he was crucified on a cross. Jesus' willingness to engage in the kind of behavior that he must have known could lead to his death shows that he valued some things more than life itself.

Jesus' death means nothing if it is split apart from the life that led up to it. But seen as the culmination of a life lived full of God's Spirit, Jesus' death sealed the importance of his life. He died a martyr, and like that of many martyrs, his death added value and importance to everything for which he had lived.

Jesus' death is important for us only as the natural consequence of his life. Without being inspired by his life, we cannot be helped by his death. Without understanding his convictions and being moved by them, his death is without meaning. But to the extent that we are touched by him and because of him feel led to cast aside the conventional wisdom of our day and to live as God would have us live, then Jesus' death is full of significance.

What is particularly pernicious about the popular understanding of atonement—a shallow, morbid understanding—is that it gives the person who accepts it the illusion of religious security. This illusion is just enough to cause many people to believe that they have all that religion has to offer. With this false sense of security, they go about their business of career, family, and hobbies or other leisure activities blithely unaware that they are living an illusion.

Far better off are those who have no religion, who have rejected standard religiosity as pious fraud, for they at least have the possibility of becoming aware of their need for real salvation. This is why Jesus preferred the company of "lost souls" to that of respectable religious folk. Unfortunately, most religious institutions do not welcome such people. They do not want people who are searching, who ask uncomfortable questions, who do not buy the standard lines. Such people rock the boat, endanger the institution, and reveal the shallowness of all concerned.

With this understanding of atonement, we can revisit the biblical images of sacrifice, ransom, and redemption. These images certainly should not be understood literally. God did not demand that Jesus be sacrificed because of God's anger at the sins of the people. Nor did God need to use Jesus' life as a ransom to buy back the wayward humans from the clutches of Satan. Nor was God required by some higher God or principle to redeem the people from slavery to sin and death with Jesus' life. The powers of evil are within, not outside, God's power. None of these images is literally true.

The biblical authors were struggling to express their conviction that Jesus' death was important. They drew on themes from the Hebrew Scriptures to express this. Something momentous had happened. It was as if Jesus had been sacrificed, his life given as a ransom and a redemption for many. His life had transformed many people. Before they met Jesus, they had felt lost and alone. Jesus taught them that God loved them in spite of what society told them. It did not matter that they were hated tax collectors, "bad" women, or even ethnically marginal Samaritans. It also did not matter whether they were "winners" according to the conventional standards.

Neither does it matter what we look like or how we think or behave or whether our society values our existence. God loves us. For anyone whose self-esteem has suffered many blows, that is incredibly wonderful news. God is at work bringing *shalom,* the Hebrew word that means much more than peace. It means rapport with ourselves, with one another, and with life itself. God does not command *shalom* to happen. No one, not even God, coerces such profound rapport. Yet God is the force that moves the world toward this end, through a means akin to persuasion. Force is the tool of the weak. God is not weak.

Jesus was a major part of the divine design to bring *shalom* to the world. Through the example Jesus set, his opposition to the conventional wisdom of his day, and the simple (though not simplistic) truths he taught, the divine Spirit gave powerful expression to the fundamental spiritual realities necessary for human happiness and fulfillment. The effects of Jesus' life, sealed by his death, are still being played out two thousand years later.

Contemporary biblical scholars emphasize that everyone brings his or her life experiences to the Bible and to the theological enterprise. We see through the eyes and hear through the ears of our own life situations and times. Each generation must grapple with the religious traditions bequeathed to it and find ways of making them alive in the present day.

My understanding of atonement has been shaped by being a child of the 1960s for whom the civil rights movement and Martin Luther King Jr. were extremely significant. King lived his conviction that all humans are brothers and sisters regardless of the color of their skin. He ultimately paid for that conviction with his life. King's life and death sealed the truth of racial equality, a profound echo of the truths of Jesus' life and death.

Martin Luther King Jr. was not only a minister. He was also deeply influenced by the writings of the Indian Mahatma Gandhi, who in turn was inspired, at least in part, by Jesus. Gandhi, too, died a martyr's death, having led the fight for India's independence from Britain. (He was assassinated by a fellow Indian who opposed his religious views.) Thus, one of the ways in which Jesus' life has continued to affect generations after him is through his inspiration of Gandhi and King.

Truth is powerful, though it often seems weak. Jesus, as well as Gandhi and King, was killed. Yet the life that Jesus led for a few short decades continues to be a light to a shadowed world. A small candle lights up a whole room. And, although small candles can be blown out, the light that is shed from a single candle metaphorically lights other lamps. Evil is real, very real. It hurts; it maims; it kills. Yet just as shadows are dispelled in a second by the lighting of one small candle, so evil disappears when confronted by the power of good.

It is clear that in the human sphere this confrontation takes years, indeed generations, to be accomplished. We humans are a slow crowd. Strangely, after an evil has finally been eradicated, it is often forgotten so gladly and quickly that people find it hard to believe it ever held sway. Evil begets evil until the chain is broken by redeeming, forgiving good.

Not that long ago in America and much of the rest of the world, it was considered improper for women to speak in public. Now, though the battles for women's full equality are not over, few remember the days when women were thought incapable of speaking in a public forum. Similarly, the day will come when African Americans, European Americans, Asian Americans, and Hispanic Americans will have trouble imagining they were ever anything other than one another's brothers and sisters. Jews, Christians, Muslims, Buddhists, and Hindus will someday see how closely related we are to one another.

This may seem far afield from what Jesus came to teach. In reality it is very near the heart of his teaching. Jesus' circle of friends included the marginal and eccentric people of his day. That was not accidental. He taught that God loved them just as much as God loved anyone. Because they were deprived of society's esteem, they were in a better position to understand God's love than some others. Liberated by that message, they took the truth Jesus espoused and spread it around the world.

Centuries later Gandhi read about that truth and appropriated it for those suffering under British hegemony. He in turn was part of the inspiration that helped King galvanize the African American community to fight for equal rights. This is what atonement is all about: giving vision to those without, offering mobility to those who are physically challenged, and making a place in society for those who are excluded.

Yet if we are not careful, we can fall into another theological hole. We can become so enthralled with the importance of such liberation movements that we believe that all we have to do is jump on the bandwagon and help the homeless, the AIDS victims, and so on to find our salvation. Doing the right things cannot save us from our sense of unworthiness, as Martin Luther knew only too well. Rather, God must first touch us and transform our lives. God must lead us to understand how God is working in our world and what God wants us to do. If we jump into whatever trend is popular, no matter how right it may be, without a deep grounding in God, we will not find the wholeness that we desire, nor will we probably do much real good.

Many people are eager to serve in soup kitchens to assuage feelings of guilt but are unwilling to examine their lives to see whether their lifestyles—their choices of where

to live, where to send their children to school, and so on—
are part of the problem that is creating the need for soup
kitchens in the first place. Soup kitchens are necessary and
good as long as homelessness prevails, but in the long run
what is needed is people who are willing to take a long look
at their own lives and who are willing to seek God's direction for every aspect of their existence.

God wants to touch each of us. God wants to assure us
that God really loves us. God also wants to enlist us in the
moral and spiritual battles of our times. For this to happen,
we must wrestle with the powers that dominate our world.
We must seek to understand them before we can do battle
with them. There is no such thing as cheap grace.

God may be calling us to help the homeless. God may
be calling us to enter government service. God may be calling us to be religious professionals. God may be calling us to
be artists. God may be calling us to be plumbers. God is calling each of us to make moral choices in every area of our
lives.

Life is not simple, and neither is the business of working
out our salvation. God bestows it as a free gift, but it is a gift
that we must actively participate in receiving. We cannot
receive it by paying lip service to creeds or confessions, helpful as these may sometimes be in articulating a certain understanding of religious truth.

God called God's child, Jesus, to attack the religious
problems of his day. Jesus accepted the challenge and in so
doing gave us a model we can emulate today, not by slavishly
imitating Jesus but by following his general approach. We,
too, are called to be the sons and daughters of God, to em-

body God's *Logos* (divine word) or, to use feminine imagery, God's Wisdom, *Sophia* (Greek for "wisdom").

There is a spark of the divine in each of us. This is what the creation story in Genesis 1 says when it tells us that God made humanity in God's image. This is what Psalm 8 reveals when it says that God made humans only a little lower than the angels. Each of us is the creation of a master artist. We reflect the spirit of the one who made us. Jesus was one of God's artistic masterpieces—for me, the supreme masterpiece—but each of us is a picture painted by the divine hand and is therefore precious.

Yet each picture is not a completed work at birth. The picture is painted throughout our lives. We can contribute to the work, or we can hinder it if we resist God's initiatives toward us. One of the paradoxes of religious thought is that God must save us by showering divine grace upon us, waking up our souls, cleansing us of our sense of unworthiness, transforming our lives.

At the same time, God seems to prod us to move toward God. The result is the awareness on the part of our awakened souls that without God's amazing grace we would be dead. Yet we also know that we have struggled and worked hard to accept the grace that God has so graciously extended to us. There are things we can do to be ready for God's grace (as the Methodists have always emphasized), but God's grace cannot be manipulated (as those in the Reformed tradition have stressed); it is God's gift.

Thus, atonement is not magic. It is not simple. It is, real, potent, and profoundly significant. God's amazing grace does touch human beings, does make us aware of our predicament and God's solution, and does transform us into powerful agents of God's love for all creatures.

Questions for Reflection and Discussion

1. What is your understanding of faith? Where and when did you learn it?

2. Did you have experiences in your childhood or youth in a religious community that you found difficult to understand or accept? If so, what were they, and how have you dealt with them as you have matured?

3. How did your childhood experiences of religious instruction affect your spiritual life? What was positive and what was negative?

Additional Resources

W. R. F. Browning. "Faith." In *A Dictionary of the Bible,* 131–32. Oxford: Oxford University Press, 1996.

William Ellery Channing. "Unitarian Christianity." In *Three Prophets of Religious Liberalism: Channing, Emerson, Parker,* edited by Conrad Wright. Boston: Beacon Press, 1961.

F. W. Dillistone. "Atonement" and "Redemption." In *Westminster Dictionary of the Bible,* edited by Alan Richardson and John Bowden, 50–53, 487–88. Philadelphia: Westminster Press, 1983.

Louis Fischer. *The Life of Mahatma Gandhi.* New York: Harper and Row, 1983.

J. P. Mackey. "Doctrine of the Trinity." In *Westminster Dictionary of Theology,* edited by Alan Richardson and John Bowden, 581–89. Philadelphia: Westminster Press, 1983.

Richard A. Muller. "Persona" and "Prosopon." In *Dictionary of Latin and Greek Theological Terms Drawn Primarily from Protestant Scholastic Theology,* 223–27, 251. Grand Rapids, Mich.: Baker Book House, 1985.

William G. Rusch. *The Trinitarian Controversy.* Philadelphia: Fortress Press, 1980.

Conrad Wright. *The Beginnings of Unitarianism in America.* Boston: Beacon Press, 1955.

Frances Young. "Sacrifice." In *Westminster Dictionary of Theology,* edited by Alan Richardson and John Bowden, 516–18. Philadelphia: Westminster Press, 1983.

· Two ·

THE DANGERS OF THE CROSS

Years ago, when I was an associate minister in suburban Virginia, the senior minister was doing a Lenten series on the cross. The titles for his sermons were "The Gifts of the Cross," "The Marks of the Cross," "The Lessons of the Cross," and "The Shapes of the Cross." Except for his last sermon, on the shapes of the cross, the sermons the senior minister gave were not as much about the pictorial image of the cross as about what the cross symbolizes: Jesus' death and the Christian life. That might seem like a subtle difference, and in a sense the distinction is subtle, but it is important nonetheless.

When the senior minister asked me to preach one sermon in this Lenten series, I had not given a great deal of thought to the cross symbol, but I was vaguely uncomfortable with it. As was often the case, writing a sermon forced me to explore and then to articulate my beliefs. At first I was stumped as to how I could fit a sermon into his series, but then it occurred to me that no series on the cross would be complete without a sermon on its dangers.

The cross is such a ubiquitous symbol today that few Christians are aware that it was not always so. An important chapter in the history of the Reformed wing of Protestantism was written by men and women who fervently believed that the symbol of the cross should not be used at all. One evidence of this is in the architecture of some of the oldest Reformed church buildings. For example, the Old Meeting House in Alexandria, Virginia, is one of the oldest structures used for Presbyterian worship still in existence today. In it, there is no ornamentation of any kind, which means that no cross is displayed.

The American flag, an important part of the American political heritage, has been affected by this same religious opposition to the use of the symbol of the cross. The reason that our flag is composed of stars and stripes and no cross is not the separation of church and state (a concept developed after the flag was designed). Rather, it was probably a result of the concern of our forebears regarding superstitious attitudes toward the cross. As early as 1635, Roger Williams advocated cutting the cross out of the British flag. He was not motivated by anti-Christian sentiments. Quite the contrary. The controversy that Williams's position created made clear that the colonists needed a flag that represented their unique blend of religious and political beliefs. When the first American flag appeared in 1775, it had no cross, unlike the flags of all the countries from which the American settlers had come.

Modern readers may well ask what superstitious views the colonists were disturbed about. Beginning in the time of the Roman emperor Constantine, it was believed that if the cross was carried into battle, for example, on a flag, then victory was guaranteed. Before an important battle Constantine is supposed to have had a vision of the cross accompanied by words (probably originally in Greek rather than Latin) that became his motto: *In hoc signo vinces,* "Under this sign you shall conquer." The vision was probably a pious fiction intended to smooth the mass conversion of the Roman Empire to Christianity, but it had a major impact on Christian art and architecture. The belief that carrying a cross into battle insured success is reflected in hymns we still sing today, which we now understand spiritually rather than literally:

> *Stand up, stand up for Jesus, ye soldiers of the cross.*
> *Lift high his royal banner, it must not suffer loss.*
> *From victory unto victory, his army shall he lead*
> *Till every foe is vanquished and Christ is Lord indeed.*

And again:

> *Onward Christian soldiers, marching as to war,*
> *With the cross of Jesus going on before.*
> *Christ the royal master leads against the foe.*
> *Forward into battle, see his banners go.*

If a cross carried into battle was supposed to insure military success, a cross worn around one's neck was supposed to ward off evil spirits.

Although the Puritans and early American Presbyterians were deeply offended by such superstitious uses of the cross, there was probably a more profound reason that they opposed the use of the symbol of the cross: the Second Commandment, which forbids images and representations of anything on heaven or earth for religious veneration. The commandment is found in two versions, one in Exodus 20:4 and the other in Deuteronomy 5:8. In both versions, technically what is prohibited, first of all, is making and worshiping idols, that is, statues representing a deity. Idols were the principal spiritual danger in ancient Israel. The commandment goes on, furthermore, to prohibit making representations of anything in heaven or on earth. The Hebrew of the relevant portion of Exodus 20:4 literally means, "You shall not make for yourselves idols or any representations of [anything] which is in the heavens above or on the earth below or in the waters under the earth." Many Christian and Jewish commentators understand these words to mean that idols shall not be made in any form. They may be right. Only the Muslims interpret the commandment literally. They allow no pictures, religious or otherwise. But by way of compensation, they have developed the most elaborate, beautiful, decorative writing of any group.

Christians have differed among themselves in their interpretations of the Second Commandment. Roman Catholics have emphasized what for Protestants and Jews is the Third Commandment, which condemns *bowing down to* or *worshiping* idols. Indeed, the Catholic enumeration of the Decalogue leaves out the Second Commandment entirely and divides the last commandment (by Jewish and Protestant counting) into two commandments. From the Catholic perspective, it is acceptable to make a picture of God, as, for example, the famous picture of God on the ceiling of the Sistine Chapel, as long as people do not worship the representation.

Protestants have traditionally banned all pictorial representations of God. The more radical Protestants, such as the American Puritans and early Presbyterians, avoided the use of visual aids in general in worship and other religious settings. Their attitude was in accord with the intention behind the Second Commandment as it is revealed in the prologue to the Decalogue in Deuteronomy 4:12: "Then the Lord spoke to you out of the fire. You heard the sound of words but saw no form; there was only a voice."

The most likely reason for the prohibition against graphic representations of the divine is that God revealed the divine will not in visual images but in words and actions. We come to understand who God is not through static images, no matter how beautiful, but through God's communication to us in words and through God's actions in history. Whenever we try to reduce to a finite picture the ineffable, infinite mystery of religion, there is a strong tendency to trivialize it and ultimately to undercut the very reality we are trying to represent. Our pictures of God always turn out to be "too small."

Our verbal "pictures" of God are also too small. Since God is infinite and we are finite, we must always speak by analogy. We say God is Father, but we do not mean that God is literally a man or physically begot us as children. Originally, the metaphor probably referred primarily to the authority of the father in a patriarchal society.

Jesus taught people to say "Father" primarily as a sign not of respect or fear but of intimacy. Thus, today when we say God is Father, we tend to mean that God is like the most loving human father we can imagine. We emphasize God's love more than God's authority. Thus, human words have a certain malleable quality that makes them more dynamic than pictorial images, which tend to be more static. Words are not without their own set of problems, as we will explore later, but they are better suited to communicating complex, subtle ideas than pictures are.

Colossians 1:15 might appear to be an exception to the Second Commandment prohibiting images. Paul writes that Jesus is the image of the invisible God. What he means is that when we "look" upon the man Jesus, we see what God is like—not in appearance, but in effect and nature. Of course, today we cannot see Jesus with our eyes (nor could Paul), but we can form a mental image of him based on the biblical record. In Genesis 1 we read that all human beings are made in the image of God. What this seems to mean is that God has given us intelligence and moral judgment. Each of us bears God's stamp, for God made us. But in a unique way Jesus is God's image.

An artist may paint many paintings. Each painting reflects the painter. But if the artist has produced a masterpiece, it towers over the other paintings, uniquely testifying to the genius of the artist. For Christians, Jesus is God's masterpiece, in whom we see the perfect reflection of God's love and truth and justice. Jesus is thus the image of the invisible God. This image, however, is not anything that could be captured on a canvas. It has nothing to do with the color of his eyes, the size of his nose, or the complexion of his skin, although Jesus' appearance is a matter of some interest, which we will consider later.

How does this relate to the Second Commandment, which prohibits images of God? First of all, Jesus is obviously not an image made by humans. In a way Jesus is God's answer to our desire for an image of God that we can see, even though we must see him today through eyes of faith. But once we try to capture the essence of Jesus in a portrait, we are in danger, because our vision can never be complete. Visual images are easy for us to grasp; thus their wide appeal. But they are almost too easy. Many people don't like to see a movie based on a book before they read the book, because usually the movie is shallow and distorts the message of the book. Rarely is the movie better than the book. It is less work for the viewer, but what the viewer receives is also less rich, less complex, and less satisfying. Furthermore, once images have been imprinted in our brains from visual depictions, it is hard to replace them with truer images. Indeed, the portraits of a blond-haired, blue-eyed Jesus that I saw early in life have stayed with me, even though I know they do not reflect either the physical appearance or the spiritual depth of Jesus.

In a similar way, some of the pictures of God that I saw as a child took many years for me to overcome. These artistic renderings depicted God as an old Jewish sage with a long beard, much like Michelangelo's God on the ceiling of the Sistine Chapel. At some point I realized that God was not an old man with a beard, but I found it very difficult to replace this discarded image with anything else. I tried to imagine God as the spirit of love, but that was too vague. Then one day, after I had preached a sermon in which I mentioned my difficulty with images of God, a member of my congregation came up to me and shared her favorite image of God. It was the beautiful racehorse Secretariat. That may seem odd. She certainly did not believe that God is a horse. What she saw in that image from nature, however, was grace and beauty and power. These attributes, raised to the nth power, are divine.

With that breakthrough, I began to see images of God everywhere—in saintly people and in the beauty of nature. I never equated God with these images, but I could grasp in these concrete lives and natural wonders something of God's incredible nature. The images of divinity that I see in life, however, are not the kind of thing that I could render with paint. I could paint the sunset, but the vision of God's glory I see in the sunset could never really be captured or communicated to anyone who saw my painting, even if it was a masterpiece.

It is not that I dislike art. To the contrary, I have always loved to draw and paint, and I enjoy various forms of art a great deal. Perhaps it is because of my love of art that I am also aware of its limitations. The visual arts cannot, by their very nature, portray deep religious truth. It took me a long time to appreciate medieval art for this reason. I found it offensive from a religious point of view, but I have come to enjoy its vibrant colors and primitive forms. The difficulty of portraying religious truth in pictures is a real problem in religious education. We must use pictures to illustrate Bible stories with young children, but I am never very happy with the quality of the graphics. They often seem very cutesy. Part of this has to do with budget constraints of curriculum producers. Part of it, though, is related to the inherent limitations of visual art.

What does all of this have to do with the cross? Primarily we should make a distinction between the metaphor of the cross and the pictorial symbol. There is nothing in the Second Commandment that forbids verbal metaphors. The Bible is full of them. Jesus is the first person reported to have used the cross metaphor. He applied it to his followers, saying that we must take up our crosses and follow him. His insight has often been trivialized by those who view physical imperfections or personal problems as their crosses. What Jesus was saying was that his life represented the pattern we all should follow. Paul also used the metaphor of the cross, but with the emphasis on what God did for us through the cross, reconciling all creation to God's self.

As opposed to the verbal metaphors that Jesus and Paul used, the two lines intersecting at right angles that are the pictorial symbol of the cross convey nothing without interpretation. Even when they are understood to refer to the fact of Jesus' execution, the meaning of this event must be supplied. How the cross came to be *the* Christian symbol is an interesting story.

In the early years of Christianity, the fish, not the cross, was the chosen symbol of Christians. The Greek word for fish, *icthus,* was an early acronym representing the Greek words for "Jesus Christ, son of God, savior." Thus, this pictorial symbol was really an abbreviated verbal creed. Because of the vagueness of the cross symbol, as we have seen, it has taken on some superstitious meanings that we now repudiate.

What does the cross communicate today? It has become associated with the popular but shallow and twisted theology that Jesus is God and that he died for our sins and that all we have to do is accept those statements and we have our free ticket to heaven. Thus, the cross symbol for many people represents a shallow, twisted theology that is a parody of the truth. Without an understanding of the pattern of life Jesus revealed to us, which involves our taking up our own crosses to resist evil as Jesus did in response to God's love for us, what God did through the life and death of Jesus cannot take effect.

Again, we see the powers of evil taking what appears to be a pious symbol of the faith and twisting it into a parody of sound theology that misleads the naive and unsuspecting. This is one of the most serious of the modern dangers of the cross. This version of a superstitious understanding of the cross may appear more subtle than the medieval form, according to which people thought that the cross could win battles for them or ward off evil spirits or vampires, and it is. We live in a more sophisticated age. If the powers of evil are going to be successful in their twisting of the truth, they are going to have to be more sophisticated in their approach than they were centuries ago. We, in turn, must be that much more vigilant against Satan's cleverness.

The symbol of the cross, with its various forms and shapes, suffers from the same problem that thwarts all attempts to portray religious truth in graphic representational form. It does not convey the heart of Jesus' message, nor even the essence of what God was doing in Christ. These we must seek with our minds and hearts in God's Word. It is here and only here that we will find the answers to the burning questions of our lives.

John Bunyan, author of *Pilgrim's Progress,* epitomizes the classic Protestant attitude toward the cross when he has the main character, Christian, arrive at the foot of the cross. Christian's burden falls from his back and he says:

> *Blest cross, blest sepulchre!*
> *Blest rather be*
> *The man that there was put to*
> *shame for me!*

What counts in the final analysis is not what we think of the cross but how God through Jesus has changed our lives.

A second problem with the cross symbol is related to the first. Because the cross is associated with a particular, narrow theology that parades itself as the *true* Christian theology, it excludes those who find it hard to swallow its irrational claims. This is especially ironic because Jesus went out of his way to include in his circle of followers those whom the religious establishment of his day excluded. It is even more ironic, and downright tragic, that this theology especially excludes Jews, Jesus' own people and the people with whom he was most concerned. He did not come to ask them to believe that he was God or to promise that if they believed he would die for their sins, they would be saved. All of those ideas came later. He came to redirect them to the essence of Judaism, love of God and neighbor.

A dear friend of mine, Helen Leneman, is a Jewish cantor and biblical scholar. Recently she was invited to sing at a worship service at Wesley Theological Seminary, a Meth-

odist divinity school in Washington, D.C. She accepted the
invitation and was warmly received, but she told me later
that she felt a little bit awkward standing in front of the huge
cross that hangs on the front wall of the chapel.

That cross excludes Helen in a way that none of the
Jewish symbols of faith exclude me. When I visited her Re-
constructionist synagogue and the Torah scroll was paraded
up and down the aisles, no one would have stopped me from
kissing it as others did. In fact, neither Helen nor I feel comfortable kissing the Torah. It feels a bit idolatrous. However,
not the Torah nor the menorah (a candelabra used at Hanukkah) nor the dreidel (a spinning top on which a Hanukkah
children's game is based) excludes me the way the cross excludes Helen, and that makes me sad. At least she knows that
not all Christians have the same theology and that some of
us warmly embrace her and her religious traditions.

The cross symbol not only excludes Jews, it also tends to
put off religious seekers from Christian and other traditions
who are not satisfied with pat answers. They assume that all
that Christianity has to offer is an anti-intellectual, even anti-
spiritual message that makes no sense to them. They quickly
move on to explore other religious traditions that are more
sympathetic, including some cults that lead down very dangerous paths. The very quality of the cross that makes it popular with many Christians—its illusion of simple, but really
simplistic, answers to life's tough questions—is the quality
that makes it repugnant to those who most need what true
religion has to offer.

Thus, the devil twists and turns, diverting seekers from
the truth by twisting it into something it is not, something

that masquerades as the truth but is a hollow shell. Not only does this mislead those who do not see through the masquerade, but it also misleads those who do by making them think there is nothing more to religion. What an upside-down world this is. The symbol that most people associate with religion represents in many cases its opposite. The real thing is simple but not simplistic. It cannot be reduced to a pictorial symbol. It cannot be drawn, painted, or sculpted. It can be grasped by the human spirit, but only with the aid of God's Spirit guiding us to it, helping us to avoid the traps set up for us by the powers of evil. The truth is simple but so elusive. God loves us, and in response to God's gift of life and love, we are led to love God and neighbor in ways that involve taking up our own crosses, that is, committing ourselves to resisting the evils in our society, just as Jesus did in his.

Questions for Reflection and Discussion

1. What religious pictures, if any, do you remember from your childhood or youth? How did they affect your faith? Were they helpful or harmful?

2. What symbols are used in your religious community? What do they represent? Be specific. Do you find them helpful, neutral, or negative? Why?

3. Have you seen any motion pictures on biblical themes? Were they helpful to your faith? Why or why not?

Additional Resources

Edwyn Robert Bevan. *Holy Images: An Inquiry into Idolatry and Image Worship in Ancient Paganism and in Christianity.* London: Allen and Unwin, 1940.

Carlos M. N. Eire. *War against the Idols: The Reformation of Worship from Erasmus to Calvin*. Cambridge: Cambridge University Press, 1986.

J. J. Stamm, with M. E. Andrew. *The Ten Commandments in Recent Research*. 2d ed., 81–89. London: SCM Press, 1970.

Henry Dana Ward. *History of the Cross: The Pagan Origin, and Idolatrous Adoption and Worship of the Image*. London: Nisbet, 1872; Washington, D.C.: Library of Congress Photoduplication Service, 1983. Microfilm.

· *Three* ·

Words, Words, Words

*T*went to a large public high school in Burlington, North Carolina. Walter Williams High School, a red-brick monolith, still takes up the city block that it occupied when I was a student. A huge grassy yard lies in front, and a parking lot in the rear. To the side is the football stadium, the center of student life. I was a member of the Boot Girls, a group that performed routines at half-time during football games and marched in the annual Christmas parade. Except for that peculiarity, I fit in with the small studious crowd whose main extracurricular activities were organizations such as the National Honor Society.

I did well in all my courses, but I always found math my easiest subject. I took precalculus my senior year and calculus in college. Numbers are very specific; they follow rules that are reasonable. They are not fuzzy. I guess I was comfortable with math because my mother had been a math major and my father was an engineer. But in spite of my affinity for math, I was more drawn to my classes in English literature. The questions that the books we studied addressed interested me in a way that the numbers of mathematics could not, even though my mind was not nearly so adept with words as it was with numbers. Words are inherently difficult. They cannot be pinned down the way numbers can. Yet I loved the challenge of making sense of them.

In the musical *My Fair Lady,* Eliza Doolittle, exhausted from elocution lessons, sings, "Words, words, words, I'm so sick of words." Her frustration with words springs from a different source than mine; nevertheless, I can identify with her sentiment. If pictorial symbols have inherent dangers so great that we should generally avoid them, we also need to be very careful about human words. Words are a better medium for communicating complex realities than pictures are. However, they are not immune to being twisted in dangerous ways.

Depending on the context, words may take on different meanings. For example, the phrase "run into" may suggest a physical collision, as in "The car ran into the fence." It can also mean an unanticipated meeting, as in "Mary ran into John downtown yesterday." Only those who are attuned to the subtle variations in meaning can successfully navigate such confusing language. Other difficulties arise from what is not said. For example, when in the book of Esther (1:11) the king demands that Vashti appear with her crown on at his drunken party, are we to understand that he is asking her to wear only her crown or to be fully clothed? The text is not clear.

Over time words change meaning. When in the King James Version of the Bible Jesus says, "Suffer little children to come unto me" (Luke 18:16), it does not mean that Jesus expected the children to be in pain. "Suffer" means "permit" in Elizabethan English. Similarly, the word "ghost" in the phrase "Holy Ghost" is not meant to suggest a pious Casper. "Ghost" is a synonym for "spirit," which could be used of an individual or of God.

Words also may have different meanings in different regions or different contexts. For example, in the South in the early part of the twentieth century, the word "dope" meant "soda," a carbonated drink. In the North it referred to an illegal drug. Today, depending on the context, the word "coke" may refer to a popular soft drink or to an illegal drug. Among some groups of teenagers, the word "bad" can mean "good." All of these variations create the possibility of misunderstanding, even among people who are native English speakers. Written words present greater difficulties than spoken ones, because the cues of body language are not available to help the reader understand the author's intention. In addition, the greater the gulf between cultural contexts, the greater the possibility for misunderstanding. The devil loves nothing better than to exploit these possibilities.

THE LORD'S SUPPER

An important example of this problem is found in the words of institution for the Lord's Supper. When I was a child, my church celebrated communion exactly the number of times stipulated in the Presbyterian *Book of Order* as the minimum, that is, once per quarter, or four times per year. That was fine with me, because I found the ceremony somewhat boring.

When I began work as a minister at Providence Presbyterian Church in Fairfax, Virginia, I was surprised to discover that the church had communion monthly. Now I had a new reason to be uncomfortable. In the Reformed Protestant tradition the sacrament is supposed to be accompanied by preaching so that people will not misunderstand the ceremony, in other words, so that people will be sure not to understand it as the Roman Catholics and, to some degree, the Lutherans do (involving, respectively, transubstantiation—the doctrine that the communion elements become Jesus' body and blood—and consubstantiation—the doctrine that Jesus is actually present with the elements), and so that people will understand communion as a symbol of God's grace. Aside from the denominational theological politics in the Reformed approach, it makes sense to articulate what we think we are doing when we engage in ceremonies the meaning of which is not self-evident. Ceremonies, like symbols, are easily misunderstood.

But how is a minister supposed to say something fresh and new about communion on a monthly basis? Fortunately, I rarely preached on communion Sundays, so the problem was more theoretical than practical. Recently, however, some new research has thrown important new light on what Jesus intended when he instituted what we call the Lord's Supper.

When Jesus drove out of the Temple merchants who were selling animals intended for sacrifice, he did so, at least in part, out of a conviction that the crass commercialization of religion was wrong. Sacrificial animals should be raised at home, not bought at the Temple. But in an urban society, the market approach had arisen to respond to a practical need. Jesus probably believed that the system put a heavy burden on the poor. That is why he quoted from Jeremiah's famous Temple sermon, calling the Temple a "den of robbers" (Jer. 7:11; Mark 11:17; Matt. 21:13; Luke 19:46).

Because Jesus thought that the Temple worship and, along with it, the sacrificial offerings of his day had been corrupted and because he could not sway the religious authorities to his perspective, he apparently felt the need to provide an alternative. Jesus' communal meals were an important part of his mission, because they included the outcasts of Jewish society. In one of these, Jesus offered a new understanding of sacrifice. Over the bread he and his disciples shared, Jesus said in Aramaic, "This is my flesh." This last word in Aramaic can mean "flesh" in the sense of either meat or body.

Jesus was not saying that the bread was symbolic of his body. He meant that in place of the sacrifices he would ordinarily have brought to the Temple, he offered simple bread. This was his sacrifice, replacing the flesh of the animal sacrifices. The parallel expression that relates the cup to a new covenant in Jesus' blood may be a later theological interpretation. See Luke 22:17–20, where two cups are mentioned. The second includes the association with covenant and blood. This cup is omitted by some ancient authorities.

Jews have long questioned how Jesus, a Jew, could possibly have suggested that even on a symbolic level people should drink his blood. The very idea was repulsive to Jews. In the context of Jesus' conflict with the Temple authorities over sacrifice, his words "This is my flesh" and "This is my blood" take on new meaning.

Jesus believed that the table fellowship he shared with his band of outcasts was a sacrifice more acceptable to God than the officially sanctioned animal sacrifices. He also believed, in accordance with Isaiah 56, that the Temple was supposed to be a house of prayer for all people, but in reality many were excluded. Thus, in effect he made his dinners an alternative to the Temple. This was such a radical reinterpretation of Jewish practice that it may have been what led Judas to betray Jesus.

Over time, other dimensions were added to Jesus' original understanding of the words "This is my flesh; this is my blood." Peter's circle saw in Jesus' practice a confirmation of the covenant that was of Mosaic proportions. That is why the words were expanded to include "This is the new covenant in my blood." James's circle believed that the Passover Seder among circumcised Jews was the ideal of Jesus' fellowship. Paul broadened this idea to include all who followed in Jesus' footsteps, whether Jews or Greeks. As in the Hellenistic mystery religions, Jesus was seen as a self-giving, martyred hero whose body and blood were given for his followers.

There is truth in these understandings. There is also truth in Jesus' original meaning. We do not need to be told today that God does not require us to make animal sacrifices. The destruction of the Temple in 70 C.E. ended animal sacrifices for Jews, so today neither Jews nor Christians follow this practice.

We do need to be reminded, however, that the modern equivalents of the Temple practices that Jesus protested cry out today to be boycotted. Upstanding Jewish citizens in Jesus' day no doubt bought their sacrificial animals at the Temple and made their sacrifices, believing that participation in this ritual made them good Jews. They were not required to include in their religious circle the outcasts of their day—tax collectors, Samaritans, or women, especially "bad" women.

Similarly, how often do we contemporary Christians fall into the habit of going to church, participating in communion, even singing in the choir and serving on various committees and boards, yet do not include in our religious circle the outcasts of our day? These outcasts take various forms. If we are ultraconservative, the liberals are outcast. If we are ultraliberal, the fundamentalists are outcast. If we are politically correct, the incorrect are suspect, and vice versa. If we are rich, the poor are not welcome. If we are poor, sometimes the rich are not welcome. In our own way we are abusing the sacrament of communion just as Paul criticized the people of his day for doing.

Someone recently told me of a Japanese man who made a practice of never rejecting any view he encountered. If he could not accept a point of view, he put it on the shelf for later consideration. He believed that a grain of truth could be found in each perspective and wanted his own view of the world to be enlarged by all others he encountered.

A similar point is made in *True North* by Jill Ker Conway, the Australian-born historian who for ten years was the president of Smith College. *True North* is the story of her years in graduate school at Harvard, her marriage to John Conway, and the years she spent first teaching and then serving as vice president for internal affairs at the University of Toronto, where she worked before being invited to become Smith's first woman president.

Conway relates that on one trip back to Australia when she was flying from Sydney to her hometown, a group of Aboriginal students was on the plane. They all went to the back of the plane, and the rest of the (white) passengers avoided them. Conway, however, joined them and spent an engrossing hour listening to their stories. When she deplaned, it was clear that the other white passengers were shocked and horrified that she was fraternizing with these students.

In the Lord's Supper, Jesus calls us to put away our prejudices, not just the ones that it is politically correct to put away, but all of them. None of us is perfect, but all of us have something to offer one another. All of us want to love and be loved.

There is something about a meal that helps break down the barriers between us. For the last few years, I have participated in a Jewish women's Seder hosted by my friend Helen Leneman and her partner. In spite of my years of Hebrew studies, I had never until recently been part of a Seder. Although I knew some of the elements of the ceremonial meal, the experience outstripped my expectations. The meaningfulness of the liturgy taught me important lessons that I hope to be able to use in communion services in my own tradition, where the ceremonies often seem tired.

Jesus' probable intention in instituting the Lord's Supper has been all but lost in the theological overlay. The overlay is not entirely wrong, if understood in the right spirit. Jesus' message calls upon us to reach out to the marginal members of our community. It requires us to bear a cross. Instead of delivering this message, however, communion services tend to focus on the popular theology that piously trumpets what Jesus did for us, with little notice of what he asks of us. Yet again, the powers of evil have triumphed, obscuring the truth and parading before us a parody of the truth that can never satisfy.

PROBLEMS WITH PRAYER

Every Wednesday evening during the academic year at the Howard University School of Divinity, we have a service of worship in the beautiful art deco Howard Thurman Chapel in Benjamin Mays Hall. The building sits on a spacious, twenty-two-acre plot, which is approached down a long, tree-lined driveway. At night when the building is spot-lighted, it is a quite impressive sight. It once was the Franciscan order's Holy Name College, but a dearth of young men studying for the priesthood made it necessary for the Franciscans to sell. Their monastery still sits just up the street from us. Appropriately enough, the divinity school is located on Shepherd Street.

Mays Hall has been renovated for our use, preserving the original Franciscan piety that breathes from every pore of the building but adding an overlay of African American spirituality that blends in amazingly well. The chapel is especially beautiful, understated but elegant. In place of the original pews that faced inward, we now have movable chairs that usually face the front. These are not as beautiful as the original pews, but they are more practical, making it possible to use the room for a variety of purposes. A magnificent organ, a less-than-perfect piano, and occasionally drums and other instruments provide a rich musical backdrop for worship.

When I first returned to the divinity school, having graduated from it when it was located in a much smaller building on Howard's main campus, I was dazzled by the worship. Many times I could not suppress tears, so moved was I by the intense spirituality. This spirituality was anything but anti-intellectual, contrary to popular opinion of African American worship. It combined the heart, mind, and spirit in a way that totally overwhelmed me.

One of the things that I like about the Wednesday evening chapel services is that we hardly ever recite Jesus' famous prayer, known as the Lord's Prayer or Prayer of Jesus. It is a rare Presbyterian worship service where this prayer is not intoned in unison, complete with the words "debts" and "debtors" rather than the more common but less accurate "trespasses" and "those who trespass against us." I have always found it quite odd that this prayer is recited so frequently in public worship in Presbyterian churches. In the Matthean version (6:5–13), Jesus emphasizes three things. First, he tells his disciples to pray privately rather than in public where they will get piety points from people observing them. Second, he tells them not to heap up empty phrases; it is the quality of what the heart feels, rather than the quantity of words, that counts. Finally, before giving them his prayer as a model, he says, "Pray then *in this way.*" (v. 9a; emphasis added).

I don't know whether Jesus opposed all public prayer, but he certainly opposed public prayer that was for show.

How much of what passes for prayer in worship today is done simply because it is expected rather than because it emerges from a truly prayerful spirit? I know from personal experience that it is very difficult to lead a group of people in prayer in a truly prayerful manner. By building in many prayers in worship, we compound the difficulty. In this regard, little is much, and much may be nothing.

Finally, Jesus clearly did not regard the prayer he gave the disciples as something that should replace their own prayers. It was simply an example, a model. Surely he would be horrified to see what we have done with it. We pray it "piously" and repetitiously but often without focusing on the meaning of the words. It is so familiar that it is like water off a duck's back. It cannot penetrate our spirits. By praying it we have the illusion that we have communicated with God. Surely, we think, if we have used Jesus' own words, God must have heard us. What a dangerous illusion! Yet again, when we think we are at our most religious moments, we may in fact be sinning most grievously. Perhaps that is why Amos cried out to the people of his day to come to the Temple and sin (4:4). He knew the devil's games even before the devil had a name. It is ironic that we use Jesus' prayer to violate the very rules for prayer that he gave us.

CREEDS AND CONFESSIONS: HANDLE WITH CARE

The church in which I grew up not only said Jesus' prayer every Sunday, we also recited the Apostles' Creed. The version we used left out the words "he descended into hell," since this phrase is not based on any text in the Protestant Bible. (See the section "The Trouble with Translations," later in this chapter, for a discussion of the different canons used by the main branches of Christendom.) The church in the Washington suburbs where I ministered for many years also followed the practice of repeating the creed, but they left in the phrase "he descended into hell" and modernized some of the language. For example, they believed not in the Holy Ghost but in the Holy Spirit. To me the mindless, rote repetition was boring and offensive, a substitute for what should be happening in worship.

When I was ordained a Presbyterian minister in the old southern Presbyterian church (officially, the Presbyterian Church in the United States)—before the southern church and its northern counterpart (officially, the United Presbyterian Church in the United States of America) reunited, having split apart at the time of the Civil War—I was required to affirm that the Westminster Confession was an accurate presentation of the system of theology taught in the Bible. Since I actually considered myself a Calvinist, a rarity among Presbyterian ministers then and now, and since the Westminster Confession represents one interpretation of Calvinism, I was not entirely uncomfortable with this affirmation, unlike many of my colleagues at the time.

Nevertheless, when the old northern and southern churches reunited, I was pleased that they agreed on a book of creeds and confessions that includes the Apostles' Creed and the Westminster Confession as one creed and one confession among many. Ordinands today are required to be guided by this book rather than to affirm any one or all of the documents it contains. In this way the denomination struck a healthy balance between affirming and learning from its history, and recognizing the limits of the human words that make up the creeds and confessions.

Although religious truth is eternal and universal and the Scriptures are a witness to this truth, each individual and each generation must wrestle with the truth in order to grasp it in terms that are relevant to the particularities of its own time and place. Part of this process involves articulating in human words our understanding of the faith. We do this both to clarify for ourselves what and how we believe and to communicate to the rest of the world our convictions. This is natural, normal, and healthy. It becomes problematic only if we think that we have captured the entire essence of God's truth for all times and for all peoples in the words we have formulated. This illusion is the epitome of arrogance. We should never forget that "now we see in a mirror, dimly, but then we will see face to face."

Our creeds and confessions are always somewhat distorted. They are never perfect reflections of the truth we strive to understand, even when they are first formulated. Over time, their meaning tends to be distorted even further as the historical context in which they arose is forgotten. To make such time-bound statements the standard that a person must accept in order to be part of a religious community is foolhardy.

The Puritans understood this and therefore had no creed. The standard for membership in their congregations was much more difficult than simply assenting to a verbal formula such as the ones used by Presbyterians today (Minister: "Who is your Lord and Savior?" Members: "Jesus Christ is my Lord and Savior," etc.). People seeking church membership had to demonstrate to the members that they had experienced God's grace in their lives. They were required to witness to their faith not through their formal theology but through their trusting relationship with God. There was no required set of words; rather, in their own thoughtfully chosen phrases they gave utterance to their experience of God's marvelous grace. Since all words are susceptible to misunderstanding, this approach was not risk free. Nevertheless, through dialogue and questions and answers, the possibility for misunderstanding was minimized. The Puritans set a high and meaningful standard for church membership yet without any officially sanctioned confession or creed.

Ironically, when creeds and confessions are given too central a place in religious tradition—and especially when the same one is used regularly in worship, as the Apostles' Creed often is—they tend to squelch theological reflection. They give the false impression that all important matters of theology and ethics were decided years ago in ways that render Bible study unnecessary. They offer a kind of security blanket to those who are uncomfortable with unanswered questions and ethical dilemmas, those who don't like spiritual wrestling. Most tragically, they tend to become a substitute for the Scriptures, which are far more complex and richer than any confession or creed is ever likely to be.

In a sense, creeds and confessions are to the Scriptures as pictorial images are to religious truth. Creeds, confessions, and graphic images all have a static quality about them, a lack of flexibility and dynamism. There is a place for pictures in religious education and a place for creeds and confessions in the church, but only if we are keenly aware of their limitations and use them advisedly. Otherwise they can easily be twisted by the powers of evil into substitutions for the living truth of God's Word.

THE TROUBLE WITH TRANSLATIONS

Divinity students and other serious Bible students are often quite interested in finding the "best" translation of the Bible. Which one, they want to know, is closest to the original? They imagine that there is a perfect original text out there that simply needs to be translated into modern English. Unfortunately, there is no perfect original. The only complete manuscripts are late, and the early ones are fragmentary. None of them completely agrees with any of the others. Since scribes copied the texts by hand, errors were made in spite of the great care with which the scribes did their work.

Thus, the question students raise about the "best" translation is a very difficult question to answer. In the first place, a decision has to be made about which Bible we are talking about. Each of the three main branches of Christianity— Roman Catholicism, Protestantism, and the Orthodox Church—has a slightly different canon. A canon is an officially sanctioned group of writings. The differences between the three religious traditions lie in the first testament. The Roman Catholic first testament includes the books that are in the Greek translation of the Hebrew Scriptures. This translation, called the Septuagint, was produced by Jews in Alexandria, Egypt, before the Jewish community had made its final decisions about what would be in its canon. Thus, there are more books in the Roman Catholic first testament than in the Hebrew Bible.

At the time of the Reformation, Protestants decided that the Christian Old Testament should be the same as the Jewish Hebrew Bible, so Protestant Bibles include a shorter first testament than Roman Catholic ones do. The Protestants, however, retained the ordering of the books found in the Roman Catholic Bible. The Orthodox canon is similar to the Roman Catholic one, but it contains a few additional books.

Since human ecclesiastical institutions have decided which books are in the canon, in theory contemporary religious bodies could decide to add additional books or to delete existing books. Although this seems rather unlikely, as archaeologists discover new materials it is not outside the realm of possibility that the canon could change again. (Of course, Revelation 22:18 warns that anyone who adds to or subtracts from "the prophecy of this book" will be punished. This is often interpreted to refer to the whole Bible, but it probably should be more narrowly understood to apply only to the book of Revelation.)

But although a change in canon is theoretically possible, it is most improbable. Although the three main branches of Christendom have slightly different canons, they all accept the books included in the Protestant canon and they all agree on the New Testament books. The only disagreement is on the inclusion of certain books in the Old Testament. Although archaeologists may discover new books, these presumably were known to the ancients who made the canonical decisions. With almost two millennia of agreement on the core of the biblical canon, the chances of such a long-established consensus changing is fairly remote.

Once a decision has been made about which canon to read, the next problem is which *text* of the canon will be used. There is disagreement on which Hebrew and Greek originals should be the basis of today's translations. Some translations, such as the King James Version and some Jewish translations of the Hebrew Bible, are based on what is called the received text, a text that actually exists but is relatively late. Others, including most of the Bibles used by Protestants today, are based on an eclectic hypothetical text, in other words, a scholarly reconstruction drawing from various manuscripts, including the Dead Sea Scrolls. For the religious seeker, it actually makes little difference which text is used, but it is important to realize that the precise contents of the Hebrew Bible and the Greek New Testament are not quite as clear as most people imagine, nor is there a perfect, error-free text out there from which translators can work.

Once decisions have been made about canon and text, many problems remain for the translator. It is well known that much is lost in the process of translation, and the more distant the language and culture of the original, the more that is lost. Classical Hebrew, the language of most of the Hebrew Bible or Old Testament, is very different from modern Western languages, and the most recent examples of it are approximately two thousand years old. Koiné Greek, the language of the New Testament, is closer to modern Western languages, but the language Jesus spoke was Aramaic, a close relative of Hebrew. This in turn was translated into Greek.

Translators approach their task with various audiences in mind. Some English translations are intended for young audiences and for those who have limited facility with English.

The translators of such Bibles have had to make compromises with accuracy for the sake of understanding. No translation can be slavishly literal, because the usual word order in the biblical languages is different from English word order, and because some idiomatic expressions do not make sense if rendered literally. Most modern translators aim to express the meaning of the text rather than a word-for-word equivalence, but some are more paraphrased than others. The more paraphrased a translation is, the more room there is for the translator to be an interpreter as well as a translator. Indeed, every translation—no matter how literal it tries to be—is to some degree an interpretation of the text and thus reflects the culture and theology of the translator.

In addition to these problems, the meaning of numerous passages is obscure. Translators do the best they can, but inevitably English translations do not reflect the difficulties of the original, nor do they reflect the double meanings (such as were discussed in the earlier section on the Lord's Supper), wordplays, and humor of the original languages. The wise layperson compares a variety of English translations and thus discerns clues to where there are problems in the original. Commentaries can be helpful too, but the best ones usually are incomprehensible without some knowledge of Hebrew and Greek. So what is a person supposed to do?

THE ROLE OF MINISTERS

When I was first ordained in the southern Presbyterian church, the official title for me and all my ministerial colleagues was "teaching elder." A requirement for ordination was (and still is) knowledge of Greek and Hebrew. The now defunct term "teaching elder" and the now rather minimal language requirement are vestiges of an earlier conviction that the minister's primary role is as a teacher and interpreter of the Bible in its original languages. Since it was well understood that much is lost in translation and that, therefore, serious Bible students needed access to the original languages, and since not everyone had the time or inclination to learn difficult ancient languages, it was believed that it made sense for each congregation to employ a person who was both a person of faith and a biblical scholar. The black preaching robes that many Protestant clergy still wear today were originally academic gowns, worn not to make the clergy seem more religious but to symbolize their learning.

With the reunion of the northern and southern Presbyterians, the generic term changed from "teaching elder" to "minister." Soon, however, it became popular to recognize that all persons of faith have a ministry, as indeed they do. Now, those ministers who are ordained clergy working in local congregations are often called "pastors." This term highlights the nurturing role of the clergy rather than the scholarly one. Indeed, that is what most congregations think they want and need. They are little interested in how well their pastor learned Greek or Hebrew or how well their pastor can help them through a perplexing biblical passage. Thus, pastors who once knew Greek and Hebrew often forget it through lack of use. They are pulled in a thousand other directions.

The pastor is expected to be the administrative chief of staff of the business operations of the church, the primary organizer of the volunteers, the chief counselor in times of crisis, a frequent visitor at home and the hospital, and the organizer and participant in myriad social programs, for both church members and those outside the church. "Successful" churches are whirlwinds of activity. Pastors are usually under great stress to keep it all happening, for where there is activity, something important must be going on.

Yet mainline churches are dying. They are dying, as Hosea puts it, for a lack of knowledge of God (4:1). We are so busy being successful that we have forgotten what it means to be faithful. We try to do everything, and end up doing nothing. We are drained and frustrated, and we wonder why. Mainline ministers have little credibility in contemporary societies. They are often objects of ridicule. At best they are viewed as weaklings. They become alcoholics and get divorced in surprising numbers. Something is terribly wrong. Is it not because we expect ministers to do everything but the central task that they are or should be especially trained to perform?

Questions for Reflection and Discussion

1. Are there any words used regularly in your religious community that you do not understand? If so, what are they? Is there someone to whom you can turn to find out what they are supposed to mean?

2. Are there words used so frequently in the worship services you now attend or once attended that you ceased to listen to them very carefully? If so, what are they?

3. Are there words used regularly that you do find meaningful? If so, what are they? Reflect on how they are helpful to you.

Additional Resources

Cambridge History of the Bible. 3 vols. Cambridge: Cambridge University Press, 1987.

Ted A. Campbell. *Christian Confessions: A Historical Introduction.* Louisville, Ky.: Westminster/John Knox Press, 1996.

James H. Charlesworth, with Mark Harding and Mark Kiley. *The Lord's Prayer and Other Prayer Texts from the Greco-Roman Era.* Valley Forge, Pa.: Trinity Press International, 1994.

Bruce Chilton. "The Eucharist: Exploring Its Origins." *Bible Review,* December 1996, 37–43.

Michael S. Christensen. *C. S. Lewis on Scripture: His Thoughts on the Nature of Biblical Inspiration, the Role of Revelation, and the Question of Inerrancy.* Waco, Tex.: Word Books, 1979.

Jill Ker Conway. *True North.* New York: Alfred A. Knopf, 1995.

Douglas R. A. Hare. *Matthew.* Interpretation Series. Louisville, Ky.: John Knox Press, 1993.

Bernhard Lang. "The Eucharist: A Sacrificial Formula Preserved." *Bible Review,* December 1996, 44–49.

Daniel Migliore, ed. *The Lord's Prayer: Perspectives on Reclaiming Christian Prayer.* Grand Rapids, Mich.: Eerdmans, 1993.

· Four ·

THE CHRISTMAS DILEMMA

*C*hristmas is a rough time for ministers, and not just because it is a busy time. Ministers must learn what their congregations regard as "sacred." Some of these sacred conventions may be unique to one congregation, but many of them are shared with countless other congregations. To a large degree, the popular misinterpretation of John 3:16 and the common magical understanding of atonement are sacred conventions in American Christian culture.

Even more sacred is Christmas, the day and the season in which Christians have celebrated Jesus' birth since the fourth century. The reason I say it is more sacred is that when I explored the topic with the congregation I served outside Washington, D.C., the reaction was far more hostile than any other response to subjects I explored.

I was doing a series of adult Sunday morning classes on the divinity of Jesus or, more accurately, titles of Jesus in the New Testament. The focus was on such terms as "Son of Man," "Messiah," and "Son of God." As an afterthought I decided to include one session on the virgin birth, since it is so important to Roman Catholics.

One of the greatest shocks of my ministry was to discover how sacred this doctrine was to many people in my congregation. I had no idea that it was held in such high regard by most Protestants. Without realizing the minefield I was entering, I explained to my class that the virgin birth was a teaching better understood poetically than literally. After all, the genealogy of Jesus that traces him through Joseph suggests that Joseph was Jesus' biological father. That does not mean that the Holy Spirit was not involved, simply that God was not a biological parent.

Perhaps if I had been less dogmatic in my presentation, I would not have experienced such a strong reaction. As a matter of fact, a poll of Presbyterian ministers taken shortly before I taught the class revealed that the majority of Presbyterian ministers did not take the virgin birth literally. If I was wrong, then so was the *majority* of the clergy of my denomination.

The same people who believe that Jesus was conceived without a human father associate the title Son of God with the virgin birth. To them, Son of God means that God was Jesus' biological father. This has a certain logic to it, but it is not the meaning of the title Son of God in the Bible; there it is used to describe many humans viewed by God as God's children, all of whom have human fathers.

Even when the title Son of God is dissociated from the virgin birth, the story of the virgin birth certainly suggests that Jesus was born without a human father. Tension exists between this idea and the genealogy that traces Jesus through Joseph. The only way I know of resolving the tension is to understand the former poetically rather than literally.

Even if one accepts a literal interpretation of the virgin birth, though, this does not prove that Jesus was somehow more divine than other humans or that we other humans are denied the essence of divinity that Jesus so fully realized. The lack of a human father does not mean that Jesus was some kind of hybrid creature, part human and part divine.

Jesus was fully human. At least that was the orthodox Christian position for centuries. Christians assert that he was divine as well, or at least that God's Word dwelled in him. The "proof" of that belief, though, lies not in the virgin birth but in the quality of his life and in its influence on others and on history.

Much of the fascination with Jesus' birth comes from the birth narratives, especially the virgin birth part of the stories. Thus, the Christmas holiday is tied up in the minds of many Christians with Jesus' divinity. Jesus' birth was not just the birth of a baby; it was different, or so the popular view suggests. Much of this kind of thinking amounts to superstition, and garbled superstition at that, drawn in large measure from pagan traditions.

The point of the stories is that God was doing something wonderful and new in the man Jesus. Too much focus on the details of these stories, like too much attention on the gruesomeness of Jesus' death, distracts from the substantive central core of Jesus' life. Without that, the rest doesn't matter. We end up majoring in minors.

Another problem with Christmas traditions has to do with the day on which Christmas is celebrated. Many Christians are only vaguely aware that Jesus was not born on December 25 but that we celebrate Christmas on this date because of the desire of the early church to accommodate itself to the pagan customs of the Romans, who had special religious festivals around the winter solstice, the time when days are the shortest but are ready to grow longer again.

The date of Christmas is not as important as the substance of what happens. Many of the customs of Christmas hark back all the way to pre-Christian pagan times. The overeating, excessive drinking, mistletoe, Christmas trees, and much else can be traced to pagan fertility customs. What these have to do with the celebration of the birth of the Christchild is hard to say. Yet Christians hold on to all of these with a tenacious grip.

More fundamental than the problem of these practices is the emphasis on Jesus' birthday itself. Even Easter, which has its own set of pagan roots and which supposedly memorializes Christ's resurrection, pales in comparison with Christmas. Was Jesus' birth really more important than his resurrection, however we may want to understand the latter? Surely not. Yet, to judge by the amount of time, energy, and money spent, Jesus' birth was by far the more important event.

More fundamental still is the notion of having only one set day a year to remember certain events. If Jesus' birth was so important, why do we think about it for only one day out of the year? If Jesus' resurrection is what we claim on Easter morning, why do we talk about it so rarely the rest of the year?

The Puritans rejected the idea of a church calendar, a set of days prescribed for remembering various events. They preferred basing the emphasis in a given Sunday's worship on what was happening within the life of the congregation and perhaps the wider community. The church calendar seemed to them an arbitrary substitute for dealing with reality. There may be days in the life of a congregation when it is especially appropriate to remember Jesus' birth and the wonderful stories surrounding it. But those days usually do not fall in December.

The Puritans took so seriously the rejection of the church calendar that they would not celebrate Christmas at all. They went to work as usual, believing that the practice of Christmas was essentially pagan and un-Christian. In fact, celebrating Christmas was a crime. Years later, when the theological reasons for their practice had largely been forgotten, the Puritans were satirized by Charles Dickens, whose *Christmas Carol* has been enjoyed down to the present with little knowledge that it derides a rejection of Christmas that was originally theologically based.

By painting those who did not celebrate Christmas as unhappy souls whose motivation was penny-pinching, Dickens glossed over the serious problems that go with the popular practices surrounding Christmas. It worked well. Those who have concerns about the way we celebrate can be dismissed as Scrooges who are too cheap or too serious to enter into the fun.

When I was a child, the only days from the church calendar that my congregation celebrated were Christmas,
Maundy Thursday, and Easter. By the time I had become a
minister, Advent, Good Friday, and Pentecost were com-
monly observed, although perhaps the difference was not so
much one of time as one of place. The church calendar seems
to be more popular in the North than in the South, though
I notice that Advent candles can be seen with equal frequency now in both areas of the country.

Lectionaries, sets of prescribed biblical readings for each
Sunday, have also become popular. Green, purple, red, and
white stoles, each colored according to the seasons of the
church year, are worn by clergy, and matching fabric serves
as Bible markers and pulpit hangings. These items certainly
make worship more colorful, but few people consider the
theological implications of these trends.

In the Middle Ages most people were illiterate, and even
priests had limited education. Perhaps it was necessary then
to dictate which texts should be read, which important
events should be remembered, and which colors should be
used on a given Sunday. But in an age when most churchgoers can read and most clergy are arguably well educated, is
it really necessary for some higher authority to tell us which
texts we should preach from and which events from Jesus' life
should be the theme of a Sunday or a season? Many argue
that the lectionary forces preachers to preach on texts that
they otherwise would avoid. But the lectionaries leave out
more than they include. When will we preach on these forgotten texts? Stories of women are rare in the lectionary.
Texts from the two testaments are combined in ways that

suggest theological modes that are no longer accepted. In addition, shouldn't sermons have something to do with specific needs of the congregation? Such needs are often difficult to fit into a predetermined text. Do we really need a lectionary?

Christmas is the most sacred of all the days on the religious calendar, at least in the popular mind. Logic does not seem to enter the debate. People like to feel nostalgic, even if the price is loneliness and debt, depression during the holiday season, and dieting afterward.

Some people have tried to deal with the problems by counseling that we put Christ back into Christmas, that we scale back the consumerism, feasting, and the like, and in their place celebrate Jesus' birthday by helping the needy. Yet so strong is the pull of the "traditional" Christmas customs that few have taken seriously the call to make Christmas a truly religious holiday.

People want to go to church on Christmas Eve and see the church all lit up. They may enjoy filling a Christmas stocking for the needy or delivering a basket of Christmas goodies. But they do not want to give up their parties and their lavish gift exchanges. Clearly these things fill an important need in people's lives.

The time around the winter solstice is a difficult time for many people. Those who suffer from depression when the sun does not shine much of the time are particularly apt to feel blue. For others, the onset of winter is depressing. For still others, the coming of the end of another calendar year brings an awareness of the failure to be all they could have been. Under such circumstances we try to make ourselves feel better by turning on the lights, preparing nice food, and taking time to be with friends and family. Is there anything wrong with that?

Not as long as we don't take our partying to extremes of gluttony and drunkenness. There is nothing wrong with a good party. Jesus enjoyed himself at the wedding at Cana and even provided more wine when the supplies ran out (John 2:1–11).

This celebration goes wrong when it is confused with religion. Religion is too important to be reduced to parties, nostalgia, consumerism, or anything that tries to substitute for the real thing. Thus, the Puritans were surely right in their rejection of Christmas, even though this rejection is no longer understood. And it is not enough simply to put the "X" (the Greek symbol for Christ) back into "Xmas." Christ and Christmas are far from identical.

Even as I write, I find myself wondering whether I have overlooked something important. The cyclical seasons of the year are an important part of everyday life. Thus, it is appropriate to celebrate God's gift of spring with its new growth, summer with its wonderful vegetables, fall with its glorious colors, and the austere beauty of the winter snow. Is there not, then, some way to integrate our celebration of God's mighty historical acts with God's annual giving of the seasons?

I can see a certain correlation between the rebirth that happens in the spring and Jesus' resurrection. Similarly, the bleakness of winter can be identified with the spiritual grimness of the time into which Jesus was born. Yet there is danger in making such correlations. As awesome as nature is, God's action in human history of bringing peace and justice is on a different plane. It is a linear progression rather than an endlessly repetitive cycle. Though each snowflake is unique, snow comes each year. Jesus does not.

Some Christians may expect Jesus' second coming, but we do not expect it every December. Nevertheless, someone from Mars might have a hard time figuring that out if they based their understanding on Advent liturgies. Attempts to make the linear progression of history, even salvation history, fit into the cyclical nature of the seasons always seem forced. And making religion simply a repetitious part of nature (i.e., business as usual) denies its radical claims.

Christians and Jews, as well as Muslims and the faithful of other religious traditions, believe that God has acted in history and continues to act in history, and that is very important. That God also maintains the natural order is wonderful. To equate these two arenas of action, however, usually results in scant attention to God's continuing involvement in bringing salvation and justice to the world. We give toys to the poor at Christmas, but we leave the poor in their ghettos and ignore them most of rest of the time.

What are the implications of this behavior on a practical level? In my own life I have chosen to celebrate Christmas as a secular season. My family decorates our indoor fig tree with white lights and ornaments. When our children were younger, they wanted a "real" Christmas tree, but, having ecological concerns, they did not want a cut live tree, so we bought one of those plastic trees that looks fairly real.

Now that the children are older, they don't mind decorating our eight-foot fig tree. It's very pretty and a lot less trouble than dragging the plastic tree down from the attic! We buy and make gifts, visit family, and enjoy seasonal taste treats. For years one of my daughters danced in the Washington Ballet's *Nutcracker.* Thus, Tschaikovsky's music is more likely to be heard at my house than Handel's *Messiah,* although I love Handel's Christmas music too.

On Christmas Eve for the last few years, my family has enjoyed a wonderful potluck party at the home of family friends whose religious heritage includes Judaism and Lutheranism. It is one of the highlights of the season. The adults gather upstairs, and the children enjoy themselves downstairs. Everyone brings nice food, and we have a lovely time. We do not sing Christmas carols or do anything else that might be identified as a religious observance.

Occasionally, although not usually in December, I meditate on the wonderful biblical stories of Jesus' birth, especially Mary's song (Luke 1:46–55), which is modeled after Hannah's song in the Hebrew Scriptures (1 Sam. 2:1–10). The theme of God's raising up the lowly and putting down the mighty does my heart good.

My convictions about Christmas forced me to alter my approach to Santa Claus. Because children often have trouble distinguishing Santa from God, and because children all outgrow Santa Claus, it seemed to me that the message we were sending in the Santa Claus myth was that God can be outgrown just as Santa is. In fact, many children now seem to "grow" in just this sad direction.

Like God, Santa brings blessings in the form of toys, or punishment in the form of switches. Like God, Santa has amazing power—the ability to deliver toys to the whole world in a single night, flying through the air in a sleigh! Like God, Santa has unlimited resources; children ask him for toys in much the same manner that many people pray to God for favors. Who but God can fill Santa's shoes? Of course, Santa Claus is a parody of God, mimicking a concept of God that is both superstitious and consumerist.

When children discover that Santa Claus is just a myth, it is a pretty logical conclusion to draw that God is also not real. Thus, from the time our children were young, we let them know that Santa Claus is just a story. It never seemed to bother them or to diminish their enjoyment of the day. They have not thrown out God along with Santa.

In part because of the years it has taken me to work through some of what I learned in church school, my children have not been regular attenders at church school and thus have less to unlearn than I did. They are interested in religious and philosophical matters. They have read the Bible from cover to cover, and we discuss theological questions together as the questions arise.

The one philosophical difficulty with our approach to Christmas is that the difference between it and the way many Christians unthinkingly deal with the holiday is subtle. One would have to observe my household closely to notice that we do not put up a manger scene or go to Christmas Eve services now that it is no longer part of my job. It would perhaps be more courageous to do as the Puritans did and thus refuse to participate in the season in any way to register my deep discontent. Yet I cannot quite bring myself to give up traditions that, viewed as secular customs, are harmless enough.

In the same way that I see no harm in participating in Christmas as a secular event, I do not see any harm in children's dressing up on Halloween as devils or goblins—although I prefer other sorts of costumes, even though I know that the Halloween customs have pagan roots. I always feel sad for children who, on religious grounds, are not allowed to don costumes and beg for candy.

A key difference, however, distinguishes Christmas from Halloween customs. Few people participate in Halloween as anything other than a secular event. Christmas, however, is different. Although many people celebrate it as a winter festival, its Christian associations are not relics of the ancient past; they are very much a part of the present. When a Christian minister decorates her household and puts lights on her fig tree, most people naturally assume that for her the celebration is a religious one.

Although refusal to decorate and to go to Christmas parties would make a statement, most people would probably read such actions as a desire to put Christ back into Christmas and to get rid of the pagan celebrations. Since that message is the opposite of the one I intend, such actions seem worse than pointless, especially when I enjoy greenery and little white lights at the time of the winter solstice.

Religion does not oppose pleasure. Religion simply wants us not to mistake mere pleasure *for* religion. As long as the distinction is made and we do not hurt others, we are free to enjoy ourselves. Thus, rather than deny myself a wholesome pleasure and send the wrong message to the world, I choose to proclaim my concerns here and in similar forums, hoping that in this way I might influence others in a positive direction.

As a minister serving a church, I struggled with how to reconcile my theological convictions about Christmas with the practices of my congregation. My concerns were not always understood or appreciated. Now, as a seminary professor, I enjoy discussing the issues associated with Christmas with my students so that they may think through the problems and make responsible choices in their lives as individuals and as servants of the church. I am delighted to find that some of them, too, struggle with these issues and that my wrestlings can help them sort through the complexities of how to live their faith in the world.

Questions for Reflection and Discussion

1. What do you like and dislike about Christmas? about Easter? Why?

2. What would you change, if you could, about the way your religious community deals with the Christmas season? What about Easter? What about other days or seasons prescribed in the church calendar, such as Pentecost, Lent, or Advent?

3. What external factors (such as family, friends, or work associates) influence the way you deal with the Christmas and Easter seasons?

Additional Resources

Stephen Nissenbaum. *The Battle for Christmas.* New York: Vintage Books, 1996.

James Taylor. "Christmas." In *The New International Dictionary of the Christian Church,* edited by J. D. Douglas, 223. Grand Rapids, Mich.: Zondervan, 1974.

· *Five* ·

LAW AND GRACE

*E*ach year I teach one section of an introduction to the Hebrew Bible or Old Testament at Howard Divinity School. Students often bring to this class stereotypes of the two testaments and of Judaism and Christianity. The most fundamental of these stereotypes has to do with law and grace. The common view is that the Hebrew Bible is a book of law and the New Testament is a book of grace. Included in this understanding is the belief that the New Testament is superior to the Hebrew Bible, because grace is superior to law. Nothing could be more foreign to either testament than this conviction, even if it is based on certain passages in the Bible or, rather, misinterpretations of these passages.

Turning first to the Hebrew Bible, we find a gracious God who chooses the Hebrew people as a special people (not based on their merits); who makes and keeps promises to them of land and nationhood; who leads them out of Egyptian bondage; who gives them the supreme gift of the law to guide their behavior; and who, like a parent, disciplines them when they go astray but always stays in relationship with them. As great as the gift of the law was to the Hebrews, prophets such as Jeremiah and Ezekiel realized that something was amiss. Jeremiah spoke of a new covenant that would be written on people's hearts, a law that would be internal rather than external (Jer. 31:31–34). Similarly, Ezekiel spoke of turning stone hearts into hearts of flesh, and of a new heart and a new spirit (Ezek. 36:26–28). The history of the Hebrew people had made abundantly clear how difficult, even impossible it is for humans to keep God's law without God's active help. Nevertheless, the problem was not with the law, it was with the people. What was needed was not a different law but a new intentionality. That is what both Jeremiah and Ezekiel envisioned, each in his own way.

Jesus did not come to annul the law; indeed, he made clear that that was not his purpose (Matt. 5:17–20). Yet he did think it important for people to understand that the essence of the law was to be found in loving God with all of one's being and in loving one's neighbor as oneself (Matt. 22:34–40; Mark 12:28–34; Luke 10:25–28). He said that all of the law and the prophets could be hung on these two principles (Matt. 22:40).

Although Jesus had no intention of undercutting the concept of divine law, he did reinterpret certain aspects of it.

In this regard he was not an innovator. Prophets before him had done the same thing. For example, although Deuteronomy 23:1–3 allows no eunuchs, Ammonites, or Moabites into the Israelite assembly, the prophet who wrote Isaiah 56, the beginning of a section sometimes called Third Isaiah, welcomes foreigners and eunuchs into the Jewish congregation, so long as they worship God (Isa. 56:3–7). It was in the same spirit that Jesus said that the Sabbath was made for humans and not humans for the Sabbath (Mark 2:27). With this as his starting point, he allowed healing on the Sabbath.

Paul took Jesus' thinking on the law one step further when he taught that certain aspects of the Jewish law, such as kosher rules and circumcision, were not incumbent upon Gentiles. He also made certain statements about the law that sound very negative but that must be understood in context. For example, in Romans 6:14 we read, "For sin will have no dominion over you, since you are not under law but under grace." It certainly sounds as if Paul is saying that the law is superseded by grace. But later Paul writes, "But now we are discharged from the law, dead to that which held us captive, so that we are slaves not under the old written code but in the new life of the Spirit" (Rom. 7:6). Here it becomes clear that Paul's concern was not with divine law but with the written Mosaic law codes that he believed had been superseded by a more perfect law. The emphasis is also on the power of God's Spirit to enable us to fulfill the demands of the ultimate law.

Paul was concerned with a combination of arrogance and hypocrisy that he believed were, for some, the loathsome underside of the Mosaic law. In Romans 2:17–24 he writes:

> But if you call yourself a Jew and rely on the law and
> boast of your relation to God and know his will and
> determine what is best because you are instructed in
> the law, and if you are sure that you are a guide to
> the blind, a light to those who are in darkness, a cor-
> rector of the foolish, a teacher of children, having in
> the law the embodiment of knowledge and truth,
> you, then, that teach others, will you not teach your-
> self? While you preach against stealing, do you steal?
> You that forbid adultery, do you commit adultery?
> You that abhor idols, do you rob temples? You that
> boast in the law, do you dishonor God by breaking
> the law? For, as it is written, "The name of God is
> blasphemed among the Gentiles because of you."

The problem was not with the law but with human reaction
to it. Rather than being grateful for the gift God had graciously given and humbly trying to live in accordance with
it, there was a tendency in Paul's time to twist the law into
a source of pride and to become so concerned with the letter of the law that its spirit was overlooked.

Paul did not disagree with Jesus about the fundamental
importance of God's eternal law. Both Jesus and Paul understood, however, the ways in which the written law could be
misused by small-minded people. They resisted these per-
versions with all their intellectual and emotional energy.
Their rhetoric was different, but the spirit of their arguments
was the same.

Unfortunately, Paul's words have in turn been twisted
into a shallow parody of what he was actually trying to say.

His misinterpreted words have become a source of Christian arrogance and hypocrisy no less profound than that against which Paul was fighting. We Christians today often take as much pride in the grace we believe God has extended to us as some Jews did in the gift of the law. Similarly, Christians often claim to be living in God's Spirit, but their behavior often belies their words. How the devil loves to do the twist.

God is a God of grace *and* a God of law. God is gracious and merciful; but God also holds us accountable for our sins. Too often Christians believe the first half of that statement but reject the second on the grounds that Christians live under grace rather than law. God is gracious and forgiving, but we are terribly mistaken if we think that God will not call us to account for our sins. Grace that does not transform us is not grace. Grace saves us by helping us not fall into sin and breaks the cycle of sin by making us forgiving instead of vengeful. It does not exempt us from the consequences of our sin.

We are making the same mistake that the citizens of Jerusalem did to whom Jeremiah preached his famous Temple sermon (Jer. 7:1–15; 26). They believed that because they were the chosen people, God would never destroy the Temple or the city of Jerusalem, no matter how badly they behaved. Jeremiah told them otherwise and nearly got himself killed in the effort. History, however, proved him correct. The Babylonians destroyed both the Temple and the capital city. Similarly, we deceive ourselves if we believe that God will not punish us when we ignore God's law. Indeed, that is why we need grace to do right and so to be saved from deserved punishment.

God punishes us as individuals and as nations. It is true that the Hebrew Bible focuses more on God's punishment of nations and the New Testament on that of individuals, but that is in part because during New Testament times, the Jews' national existence was precarious. After the Babylonian exile the religious emphasis began to shift from the corporate to the personal. Jesus announced an understanding of religion that is deeply personal instead of primarily corporate. God is concerned with us both as individuals and as nations. And as both individuals and nations, we live under God's grace and are accountable to the divine law.

THE CHURCH AND POLITICS

If God is concerned as much with our national behavior as with our individual actions, then the question arises as to the proper relationship between religious institutions and politics. In biblical times, the concept of the separation of church and state was not even a gleam in anyone's eye. Religion and politics were inextricably intertwined. The Hebrew prophets proclaimed God's Word to kings and ambassadors in their official capacities more frequently than they did to individuals as individuals.

Jesus' advice to give to God the things of God and to the emperor the things that belong to him (Mark 12:13–17; Matt. 22:15–22; Luke 20:20–26) sounds like an early version of the separation of church and state, but it was not intended that way. A group of people had come to try to trick Jesus into saying something that would get him into trouble. They asked him whether it was lawful to pay taxes to the emperor. If Jesus answered no, he would be open to the charge of treason. If Jesus answered yes, he would be unpopular with his followers, who hated the Romans. They resented these taxes because the taxes were symbols of Roman domination and because they had to pay in Roman silver coinage. These coins (called denarii) were stamped with the head of the emperor, who was considered divine, in violation of the Jewish desire not to revere anyone as sovereign other than God. In deference to these Jewish scruples, the Romans minted for circulation inside Palestine copper coins that did not bear the imperial image. But by asking his opponents for a silver denarius, Jesus forced his questioners to reveal that they were carrying Roman coins rather than Jewish ones. In this way he revealed their hypocrisy. Jesus knew that these coins were circulating freely in Palestine, and he rightly suspected that his interrogators possessed some of them. This, in effect, committed them to an affirmative answer to their own question. By accepting Roman coinage, they accepted the economic benefits and political stability conferred by Rome. His answer avoided the trap they had set for him and turned it back on them. If they were using Roman coins, why should they not pay taxes to the emperor? Jesus' answer was clever and wise, and in a sense it was a precursor to the modern principle of the separation of church and state, but that was not the point Jesus was making.

Jesus' answer, that one should give to the emperor the things that belong to the emperor and to God the things that are God's, does not mean that the spiritual and the political are two independent and wholly unrelated realms. Rather, it means that we are subject to two kingdoms, a temporal, political one and an eternal, spiritual one. Our allegiance to the former is conditional, to the latter unconditional. As long as the emperor, that is, the state, does its job of providing a reasonable framework for our common life and respects fundamental human rights, it may claim its due. If its demands conflict with our allegiance to God, that is another matter, with which Jesus does not deal directly. However, it is clear that Judaism's answer to this problem was that whenever there is a conflict between our commitment to God and our commitment to the government, God takes priority; Jesus most likely agreed, as his death illustrates. For example, in Daniel 3, Nebuchadnezzar demands that all of his subjects bow down to a golden calf, but of course, Shadrach, Meshach, and Abednego, being good Jews, refuse to bow down. They are cast into the fiery furnace, from which God saves them. Being forced to worship in a state-sponsored church would be a modern analogue to this situation. Because of the principle of separation of church and state in the United States, we do not need to fear that kind of demand from our government. This is a precious freedom, important more for the purity of religion than for the safety of the state. Religious people should be its first protectors rather than seekers to dissolve it.

Where did this idea come from? The United States was the first country in the world to proclaim the twin principles of religious liberty and the separation of church and state. These principles are so much a part of our way of life in this country that we often take them for granted. We forget that only two hundred years ago, a relatively short period of time when one considers that recorded history is thousands of years old, religious liberty was a radical idea and that the fight for its inclusion in the documents that articulate our concept of government was long and hard.

It is still a radical idea in much of the world. In other parts of the world, people are still being executed for adhering to the "wrong" faith. In Iran, for example, Baha'is are not tolerated. They are often killed. Within the lifetime of many of us, Jews were systematically exterminated in Germany.

Two streams flowed together to bring about the triumph of religious liberty in America. One of them was eighteenth-century rationalism, as espoused by Thomas Jefferson. The other stream was religious, as represented by the Baptist Isaac Backus. James Madison, who was a central actor in the drama, had one foot in each of these camps.

Before we look at the events that led to the victory for religious freedom in Virginia that presaged what would happen in the colonies as a whole, we should add that more was involved than personal religious liberty, as important as that was. The victory also involved the full institutional independence of the state from all churches and of all churches from the state. England, the mother country, and many other democracies have personal religious freedom, but they do not have the constitutional separation of church and state that the United States does. This separation was an extremely radical idea. That a nation could exist and be unified without the spinal column of an official religious establishment was not generally accepted in the eighteenth century. Even today this fundamental part of our philosophy is under attack by those who wish to institute officially sanctioned prayer in the schools or the like. I for one do not want my children exposed to the kind of sentimentalized, watered-down religion—it does not even deserve that name—that would surely result if such ideas were to hold sway. We separate church and state not because of our hostility to religion but because we believe that both religion and the state function better when they are independent of each other.

Virginia was not the first state in which full religious liberty existed. It existed much earlier in Rhode Island and Pennsylvania. But, as important as these states are in the history of religious liberty, Virginia, with its Declaration of Rights, most directly led to the inclusion of the Bill of Rights in the federal Constitution. George Mason was the chief author of the Virginia Declaration of Rights. The last item in the Virginia document, Article 16, was on religious liberty. Mason, a conventional Anglican, wrote that since reason and not force should dictate belief, "all men should enjoy the fullest Toleration in the Exercise of Religion according to the Dictates of Conscience." That doesn't sound bad now, and it probably didn't sound bad to most of the delegates to the constitutional convention. Mason was using what had become the conventional concept following John Locke's *Letter concerning Toleration* and legislation in 1689 in which the mother country had settled on limited toleration of religion after years of revolution, uproar, and regicide.

But for one delegate to the convention, Mason's wording was not nearly enough. His name was James Madison. He was very young, shy, short, inexperienced, and diffident, and his voice was weak, but he was not going to let pass mere "toleration." Although Madison was an Anglican planter's son, he had not gone to William and Mary as would have been expected, but rather up north to the College of New Jersey, later to become Princeton. This school had been founded by "New Side" Presbyterians who emerged from the revivals of the 1740s. It had become a lively center of revolutionary religious and political ideas. John Witherspoon, a Presbyterian minister, was president of the college when Madison studied there. Witherspoon had recently come from Scotland, where he had had his own troubles with the *kirk,* or church. Mere toleration, implying condescension, was disdained by Witherspoon and others with whom Madison studied. Madison had also seen religious persecution firsthand. Near Madison's home, the Great Awakening had left many pools of new believers. In activity unauthorized by the state, Baptists were meeting in homes, preaching without a government license, and doing evangelistic work in a way repugnant to the Anglican establishment and perhaps even to religious truth. As a result there were persecutions, arrests, and imprisonments.

At the Virginia constitutional convention Madison drafted an amendment to Mason's toleration article that eliminated "toleration" and replaced it with the following words: "All men are equally entitled to the full and free exercise of religion according to the dictates of conscience." The word "equally" was important. It survived into the final draft. It meant that the unlearned Separate Baptists and the well-educated Anglicans had the same rights of conscience. It was not emphasized at the time that this idea jeopardized the established Anglican Church of Virginia, but it did.

Since Madison was only twenty-five and a novice in public affairs, he had the great orator Patrick Henry offer the amendment for him. The first draft of the amendment included the clause "that no man or class of man ought on account of religion to be invested with peculiar emoluments or privileges." Someone apparently had read the words closely, for Henry was asked whether this meant the end of the established church. Henry was not one to commit himself far beyond the public opinion, so he backpedaled and said no. Whether because of or in spite of this, the amendment failed. Madison then revised his amendment, leaving out the clause. This time the conservative Edmund Pendleton offered it and it passed. Thus, the concept of "free exercise" of religion began its long path.

Madison had not achieved everything he wanted, but he had gotten much more than mere tolerance, which in English law had not extended to atheists, Catholics (implicitly), or some others. Although it is not clear that the Virginia delegates understood the full implications of what they were doing, they had removed religious freedom from the purview of what lawyers call "legislative grace," with its implicit assumption that what had been granted could be taken away, and had placed it in the domain of what is called "inalienable right." In Article 16 of the Virginia Declaration of Rights is anticipated the full disestablishment of religion and the separation of church and state.

If it was Madison who was largely responsible for including in Virginia's Bill of Rights these radical ideas, it was Thomas Jefferson, a few years Madison's senior, who was to become the foremost advocate of the new religious freedom. It is a long and interesting story how the implications of Article 16 came to be implemented, too long to elaborate here. Suffice it to say that Jefferson himself wrote later that the contest over religion in Virginia was the severest in his entire lifetime—which was saying a lot, considering all the battles in which Jefferson was involved.

Fifteen years after the Declaration of Rights was passed in Virginia in 1776, and two years after the federal Constitution was ratified in 1789, the Bill of Rights to the Constitution, the ten amendments guaranteeing various freedoms, was adopted. Now freedom from federal interference in religious matters was guaranteed not simply in Virginia but in all the states of the young nation. Madison wrote these articles.

I have concentrated on what happened in Virginia both because of its influence on the federal Bill of Rights and because Madison's role shows especially well how a combination of eighteenth-century rationalism and religiously motivated convictions brought about one of the greatest intellectual revolutions in history. Some of the partners in the story make odd bedfellows, for they include the most educated, most liberal thinkers, such as Jefferson, on the one hand, and some of the least educated sectarian religious people, on the other. Madison stands with his feet in both traditions. Well educated, Anglican, yet influenced by John Witherspoon, president of the College of New Jersey and a New Side Presbyterian, and disturbed by the persecution of Separate Baptists in his own home territory, Madison was perfectly suited to lead the way to religious liberty. Yet he was certainly not alone. And although the implementation of the new religious freedom was very difficult, we can also see, looking back, that the currents ultimately had to go this way.

In the United States we are heirs of these giants whose ideas are, for the most part, so accepted today that we cannot imagine what life would be like any other way. Yet people today often become confused and think that the principles of religious liberty and the separation of church and state mean that churches should not get involved in politics. That was the furthest thing from the minds of those who framed these principles. The separation of church and state means that the state cannot establish, endorse, or fund one religious group. Religious liberty means we are free to believe whatever we like without fear that the state will persecute us. These principles do not mean that religious bodies do not have the right to make their opinions on political matters known or that individuals may never express their religious feelings in a public forum. This is yet another twisting of the truth. Citizens have a duty to participate in the political process, and this participation may be carried out individually or in various groups, including religious ones. If our religious convictions do not shed light on the political decisions we make, then our religion is shallow indeed. Nevertheless, it is still important to raise the question of the proper relationship between the church and politics.

Governments do sometimes engage in unjust and immoral behavior. The question that bothers many people is what role the institutional church should play in addressing such situations. The Hebrew prophets frequently excoriated their nation for its social and moral abuses. After denouncing his fellow citizens for their violations of what the standards of social justice demanded, Micah once quoted one of his detractors:

"Do not preach . . .
one should not preach of such things;
disgrace will not overtake us." (2:6)

Even in those days people did not like to be challenged or criticized because of their collective failings. They didn't like to be reminded that their societal sins would catch up with them. But in spite of negative reactions, the prophets preached on, and their words have been immortalized in the Bible. They provide the biblical precedent for contemporary preachers and prophets to speak out against perceived abuses in our government's policies. So the question is not really whether the church should be involved in politics, but how, when, and under what circumstances.

The prophets spoke out of their own spiritual insight and with a conviction that God called them to do so. Similarly, sometimes in contemporary society the moral imperative is obvious and silence is shameful. We must always remember the silence of most German churches during the rise of Hitler, even if we doubt that our current society has sunk to that level. There are times when clear and serious violations of human dignity by the government absolutely require that the church as church take action. Such was the case with racial segregation. Many churches became directly involved in the civil rights movement. Their involvement was a high point in modern church history. Today some churches have felt called to oppose abortion and, although abortion is a debatable issue, if their consciences lead them in this direction, it is their right and duty to do so.

Sometimes churches may properly speak from a moral perspective on issues that are less clearly evil than the genocide perpetrated by the Nazis, the apartheid once practiced in South Africa, or the slavery and later segregation of blacks in the United States. The rise of state-sponsored gambling may be an example. It is safe to say that, whether out of the traditional Christian dislike of gambling in the pagan form of worshiping the goddess Fortuna or out of a modern Christian concern about tempting the poor to give up their needed resources in a hope that by definition must be vain, Christians must be very concerned about state-sponsored gambling proposals.

There are other times when issues arise to which the Bible speaks directly or indirectly but which do not require government action and may not require churches to take a stand. Excessive drinking is a bad thing, and churches should give guidance to their members concerning it. However, the church-led campaign to force its moral views on the population at large resulted in Prohibition, a government action that was ineffective, to say the least, no matter how well intentioned. The church was not wrong to involve itself, but it was wrong in the means it sought to use.

Then there are some issues that have moral implications but about which the answer is not yet clear. These issues should be explored within churches to get greater understanding that may eventually lead to a firm answer. Various kinds of genetic engineering research may fit into this category.

Finally, we should remember that many political issues are morally neutral. Whether a professional ball team relocates is a question about which many residents may have strong opinions, but it is not a moral issue on which the church should take a stand.

So, the relation between religion and politics is a various one. Sometimes churches must take a stand. Sometimes they may take a stand if they wish. In other matters churches should confine themselves to advising their own members, and in some cases churches should not be involved at all, not because of the separation of church and state but because the moral implications are negligible.

The importance of the principle of separation of church and state is hard to overstate. Although it is not directly derived from the Bible, its inspiration was partly Christian. It is based on God's right to rule over consciences. Its value has been proved in the two-hundred-plus-year history of the United States. But just as biblical truths are often twisted into shallow parodies of themselves, this principle also has been frequently mangled. Some believe it prohibits churches from making their perspectives on political issues known. Some think that schools should never allow students to express their religious views, even in term papers or artwork. They have turned the principle upside down. It is intended to protect churches and individual believers from government interference, not the government from criticism. Nor is it intended to limit freedom of speech. The devil loves to twist the truth. How vulnerable we are to Satan's machinations.

THE CHURCH AND MORALITY

Taking God's law seriously sometimes requires churches to criticize the behavior of governments. It also requires churches to make decisions about whom it will ordain to church office. Most denominations have different standards for ordination than for membership. In most cases all that is required for membership is the simple assertion that the candidates are Christian and intend to live a Christian life. The details of their theological and ethical convictions, as well as the particularities of their experience of grace, are rarely scrutinized. This may be an error, but it is a common one.

Candidates for ordination usually are grilled more thoroughly and are expected to have certain training. They must give evidence of their faith and their sense of call to the ministry. In some cases they must pass ordination exams to prove their knowledge and understanding of the Bible and of the traditions of the denomination in which they will serve. I came through before the written exams. My examination, in Orange Presbytery in North Carolina, was oral. The main impression I had of it was that the examiners wanted to be sure that my theology was liberal enough! I almost failed on that account. In addition, psychological tests are sometimes required. I took one that seemed rather silly. In the past it was generally assumed that unless there was evidence to the contrary, candidates were morally fit. I do not remember any questions regarding my sense of morality. Today debates about sexual behavior have focused attention on ethical standards in a highly contentious manner.

Different approaches to biblical interpretation have resulted in quite different understandings of God's law. Those who are schooled in the historical-critical method are aware of the particularities of the historical and cultural contexts in which biblical passages were first spoken or written. Not all biblical statements are viewed as timeless truths by these interpreters. A great example is the advice for women not to wear their hair in braids (1 Pet. 3:3). At different periods in history, braids have had very different meanings. Apparently, in biblical times they were considered dangerously seductive. Today in the United States, braids are worn primarily by European American schoolgirls and African American girls and women. They may be simple or elaborate, but they are not associated with inappropriate behavior. Few take seriously the biblical admonition against wearing braids today. Other admonitions that may be as culturally bound as that one, however, are viewed by some as timeless statements that we must take seriously today.

How are we to know who is right and whose interpretation should be accepted? The question is not only theoretical, it has very concrete, practical effects on people. The issue also involves matters of church law. When should churches simply give advice, and when should they take stands that exclude those who disagree?

Sometimes churches have no choice but to take stands that will anger some. For example, the issue of race is one that requires a decision one way or the other. Churches cannot sit on the fence; they must decide whether they are open to persons of all racial backgrounds or not. Similarly, churches have had to make decisions about whether to ordain women to the ministry. Race and gender are accidents of birth. They are not matters of morality. Nevertheless, some issues of biblical interpretation have affected these decisions.

Sexual orientation may be an accident of birth; sexual behavior is a matter of choice. Up until fairly recently, the vast majority of Christians probably assumed that non-heterosexual behavior was sinful. Changes in our culture and new approaches to the relevant biblical passages have called that assumption into question. Who is right, and what do we do when reasonable people disagree?

Many denominations have passed legislation that enshrines in church law one interpretation of biblical law on specific questions. The fact that these same denominations have not passed similar legislation against sins such as pride, gluttony, sloth, greed, or jealousy suggests that we are dealing with a very peculiar—and unhealthy—preoccupation. Beyond the problem of a simplistic approach to biblical interpretation, an equally disturbing problem is the rule-book mentality that is enshrined in such legislation. The idea seems to be that morality is a simple, straightforward matter to determine. It is also assumed that those who have not violated a simple set of rules are morally fit.

The frequency of clergy leaving churches because of sexual misconduct, however, shows how false the presumption of moral fitness is, even in the area of sexuality. Moral leadership includes how we handle our sexuality, but the issues are much more complex than whether one is in a sexual relationship outside of marriage. In addition, morality involves many more issues than sexuality. A serious consideration of the integrity of candidates would probably be wrenching, but it might also prevent many of the disasters that sully the reputation of churches. It is clear that a sincere concern about the moral suitability of candidates for ministry would involve thoughtful judgments for which no written legislation will substitute.

The recent Presbyterian Amendment B has solved one problem, retained another, and created a new one. It theoretically solved, at least on paper, the problem of a church obsessed with sexuality. (Whether it has addressed that problem in reality will be seen in the way the legislation is implemented.) The new legislation has retained the problem of enshrining one particular interpretation of the Bible in church law. This is contrary to the Reformed principle of freedom of conscience. This principle gives individual Christians the right and responsibility to interpret the Scriptures for themselves, using every resource available to them. Only in matters that are essential to the faith does this principle not apply. Presumably, one's understanding of the Bible's teaching on sexuality is not essential to salvation.

The new problem that the legislation has created is the great weight it gives to the Confessions of Faith. The Confessions are documents in which the churches through the ages have articulated their understanding of the fundamentals of theology and ethical behavior. Traditionally they have carried great weight in the Presbyterian denominations, but they have always been subordinate to the Scriptures. Now they are virtually ethical mandates whose weight is equal to that of the Bible. This is blasphemy.

In the past, the national Presbyterian church set broad standards for ordination within the denomination, but it was left up to the local bodies—whether the local congregation or the local presbytery—to determine whether a candidate for ordination was fit for church office. That is why this denomination is called Presbyterian! No one is without sin, but officers should be models for church members. At the local level, a candidate should be examined in a thoughtful and responsible manner to determine whether any conduct brought to light during the interview is incompatible with ordination.

The new legislation in effect stipulates a checklist of sins that are considered too grave to be acceptable in church officers, regardless of context. Yet, just as assent to verbal formulas substitutes for and cheapens a more thoughtful approach to admission to church membership, this new legislation, in its zeal to assure that church officers are morally pure, also will result in a kind of legalism that focuses on the externals rather than the inner spirit. In place of thoughtful examination, we get checklist morality. This is a new form of a covenant of works.

Surely Jesus and Paul would be appalled. Both sought to understand the inner essence of the law, and both fought against legalism. Both extended the religious community to include people who were formerly considered too sinful or too impure to participate. Both had high standards—very high standards—but their standards were thoughtful, creative interpretations of their tradition. How hard it is for us to follow in their footsteps. The forces of evil have twisted Jesus' and Paul's approach into its antithesis, and the church is much poorer as a result. It is becoming a sepulchre, beautiful on the outside but dead on the inside.

Questions for Reflection and Discussion

1. In what ways has your religious community's approach to moral issues been helpful to you? In what ways has it been harmful?

2. Does your religious community consider some sins worse than others, either in theory or in practice? If so, which ones are considered the most dangerous, and

what practical steps have been taken to deal with the problems?

3. Has your religious community taken a stand on a political issue that has serious moral implications? Why or why not? If it has, how has this stand affected the life of the community?

Additional Resources

Gordon L. Anderson and Morton A. Kaplan, eds. *Morality and Religion in Liberal Democratic Societies.* New York: Paragon House, 1992.

Lance Banning. *Sacred Fire of Liberty: James Madison and the Founding of the Republic.* Ithaca, N.Y.: Cornell University Press, 1995.

Harold J. Berman. "Law and Theology." In *Westminster Dictionary of Christian Theology,* edited by Alan Richardson and John Bowden. Philadelphia: Westminster Press, 1983.

Robert Booth Fowler. *Religion and Politics in America.* Metuchen, N.J.: American Theological Library Association and Scarecrow Press, 1985.

Ronald M. Hals. *Grace and Faith in the Old Testament.* Minneapolis: Augsburg Publishing, 1980.

William G. McLoughlin, ed. *Isaac Backus: On Church, State, and Calvinism, Pamphlets: 1754–1789.* Cambridge: Harvard University Press, 1968.

Merrill D. Peterson and Robert C. Vaughan, eds. *The Virginia Statute for Religious Freedom: Its Evolution and Consequences.* Cambridge: Cambridge University Press, 1988.

Frank Thielman. *A Contextual Approach: Paul and the Law.* Downers Grove, Ill.: Intervarsity Press, 1994.

· Six ·

Needlework, Anchors, and Blessings

$\mathcal{B}$eside the desk in my bedroom is a framed piece of needlework entitled "Religion." It is a family heirloom, having been embroidered by Susanna Baker in 1792. The material on which she worked is now threadbare, and her work is without any ornament whatsoever. Within a hexagon that she stitched as a border, she wrote a short essay on religion. We do not know whether she is the author of the words, but since she was in the Puritan tradition and the Puritans were concerned with expressing their convictions through their own carefully chosen words rather than in the verbal formulas of others, she may well be. The sampler reads as follows:

Religion, the balm of life, the anchor of hope, the dispeller of fears, the haven of rest, will carry us into the arms of him, who is mighty to save from every trouble. Defended by his shield, though afflictions spring not out of the dust, they shall not hurt us, supported by his power, though the mighty rage, they shall not prevail against us, guided by his wisdom, though snares and evils encompass our paths, we shall escape them all. In vain may be our toil for Riches to secure us; but our trust in him will never be in vain. The arrows of affliction may reach the very pinnacle of greatness, and cares and terrors climb up to us, however high we may place ourselves but he is a tower of defence, a place of refuge, a rock of salvation unto which the Righteous flee and find safety.

Expressed beautifully yet simply by these words is a deep and abiding trust in God. Susanna Baker does not even call God by name, perhaps sensing that God is beyond all of our names. (Of course, by avoiding the name of God she is forced to use masculine pronouns for God, a practice that many today try to avoid so as not to suggest that God is male. The problems with language!) The God who is the unnamed focus of Susanna Baker's essay is a God who cares about her and about all God's people.

It is this kind of trust in a compassionate God that is the essence of theistic religion. What was true in the eighteenth century, when Susanna Baker wrote, was true for the ancient Hebrews. It was true for Jesus, and it is true for us today. In every generation the powers of evil have attempted to divert people from this simple truth. They have tried to persuade us to put our trust in everything from temples to idols to foreign powers to superstition to wealth and power.

Satan has redefined faith as credulity. Atonement has been twisted into a kind of mythology that says that because Jesus was God and he died, all we have to do is assent to that idea and we have a ticket to heaven. The real message Jesus came to give us is lost in the process. That message is that God loves us, all of us, and wants us to love God and our neighbor in response to God's amazing love for us.

The powers of evil have substituted the graphic symbol of the cross, which throughout the ages has been associated with various forms of idolatry and superstition, for the living reality of God's word. Human words have been twisted in a thousand ways, obscuring Jesus' message and, like the cross, being substituted for the true spirit of religion. The Bible has been idolized, translated in misleading ways, and misinterpreted, and the ministers whose primary duty it should be to help people sort through these problems are pulled in myriad other directions and often have not received the training necessary to do this work even if they want to.

Essentially nonreligious celebrations, such as Christmas, have been hopelessly confused with religion and draw the faithful away from the true purpose of religion. God's law and God's grace have been misunderstood as antithetical to each another; the principle of separation of church and state has been twisted to imply that churches have no business concerning themselves with politics; and churches, in their efforts to maintain high moral standards, have seen the splinters and ignored the beams.

Although the devil twists and turns, God's eternal truth prevails—an anchor that prevents us from drifting too far. In each age people must rediscover the truth, sifting it out like wheat from chaff. Because each generation lives in a new historical period, its members must do their own sifting and sorting. God's truth is eternal, but the devil's twists and turns are always just different enough that new challenges confront us. Studying history gives us clues as to the devil's modus operandi, but we must still do the hard work of understanding what is happening in our own day. We do this hard work for ourselves, because we can never be free until we do. We also do it for others who may be misled by the superstitious and idolatrous beliefs that parade as religious truth. Once these deceptive mythologies have been unmasked, it becomes obvious how hollow, shallow, and absurd they really were. However, until they are unmasked they have the power to keep people away from God.

It is not only Satan that develops various deceptions to confuse us. Because of our sinful natures, we are naturally prone to avoid a relationship with God. We do not like the kind of self-examination that such a relationship requires. As a result, Satan has a fairly easy job of diverting us, because we want to be diverted, at least on one level. At a deeper level, we all have a hunger for God that nothing else will satisfy. We may try everything else out first, in hopes that a satisfying solution will present itself that will shield us from the soul-searching that true religion requires of us. In the long run, however, we discover that there is no successful shortcut. We